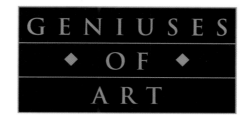

GENIUSES
◆ OF ◆
ART

GAUDÍ

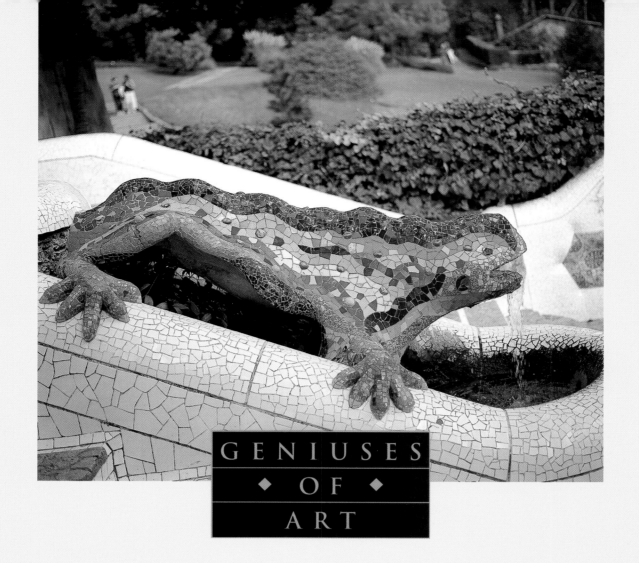

GENIUSES
◆ OF ◆
ART

GAUDÍ

susaeta

Scientific Co-ordination:
Juan-Ramón Triadó Tur
Titular Professor of History of Art at the
Universitat de Barcelona

Text:
Alberto T. Estévez
Doctor of Architecture
Director of the Technical School of Architecture,
Universitat Internacional de Catalunya

Translated by:
Carole Patton

Cover Design:
Paniagua & Calleja

CONTENTS

Biographical Notes - 7

Early Works - 15
Casa Vicens, Barcelona - 15
Casa *El Capricho*, Comillas (Cantabria) - 18
Güell Stables, Barcelona - 20
Güell Palace, Barcelona - 22

Works Outside Barcelona - 27
Episcopal Palace, Astorga (León) - 27
The Teresian School, Barcelona - 29
Casa Fernández y Andrés (Casa Botines), León - 32
The Güell Wine Cellars, Garraf (Barcelona) - 34

The Turn of the Century, On the Road to a Definitive Change - 37
Casa Calvet, Barcelona - 37
Güell Colony Church, Santa Coloma de Cervelló (Barcelona) - 39
Güell Park, Barcelona - 42
Casa Figueras (Bellesguard), Barcelona - 45

The Prime of the Genius - 49
Casa *Batlló* (*Casa dels Ossos:* «House of the Bones»), Barcelona - 49
Artigas Gardens, La Pobla de Lillet (Barcelona) - 52
Casa *Milà* («*La Pedrera*»: «the Stone Quarry»), Barcelona - 53
Sagrada Familia Provisional School, Barcelona - 56

His Life's Work - 58
The *Sagrada Familia* Church, Barcelona - 58

Arts and Crafts - 67
Stonework - 67
Woodwork - 70
Ceramics - 71
Ironwork - 74

Sources of Inspiration - 77
Chromatic Architecture - 88

Bibliography - 91

Gaudí and the Critics - 92

Alphabetical Index of Works - 95

Biographical Notes

Maybe one could think that the figure of Antoni Gaudí is the result of an unrepeatable geographic-historic context: Catalonia, a land of particular popular building traditions, at the end of the nineteenth century and the start of the twentieth, years of singular artistic-cultural changes. However, beyond this external confluence of conditions, only the tenacious will of somebody like Antoni Gaudí with every step he took could light the wick. In other words, it is easier than it may initially appear to become an eminent personage such as him. We are too often unaware of possible opportunities and allow precious moments which we could take advantage of to escape. And this occurs at any place and any time. Because Antoni Gaudí, in order to achieve the enormous concentration shown in his works, dedicated his entire life to the art of building. He did not devote himself to teaching, giving conferences, travelling, politics, writing, publishing, or to any other art, interest or work, nor did he hardly have any social or family life, something which was common for his colleagues.

Maybe this was why nobody could equal him, specifically in the field of architecture. For example, Lluís Domènech (1850-1923), besides being an architect, also worked as a school teacher and a headmaster, an historian and a politician. Josep Puig (1867-1957) was also a teacher, an art historian, an archaeologist and a politician. Or going even further, Henry Van de Velde (1863-1957), was not only a teacher and a theoretician, but also a painter, a musician, a man of letters and a designer of objects of all sorts.

On the other hand, as to family ties, Adolf Loos (1870-1933) was married four times; Otto Wagner (1841-1918) had six children, and Charles Rennie Mackintosh (1868-1928), eleven brothers and sisters. Antoni Gaudí, however, only had one sister who saw him graduate as an architect, but she died the following year, three years after the death of their mother. He never married, having only one niece who ended up dying long before he did. Neither did he carry out a large variety of works or take part in many projects or competitions, which is usual in the case of any architect, but has rather a limited number of works, amounting to about only a score. Enric Sagnier (1858-1931), for example, carried out hundreds of works and projects and Frank Lloyd Wright (1869-1959), thousands. And it could even be said that, practically, his only book was that of nature and his only show that offered to him by the Catholic religion that he lived so intensely. It was from these two sources that he would take the subject and the strength of his architecture.

Now then, it is true to say that Catalonia has its peculiarities regarding phenomena related with architecture. Maybe one of its strangest is that related to its tradition of castles. And not precisely because it is a land of castles, although we can find numerous examples dating from all periods, ranging from the earliest

Casa Milà
1906-1910/1911, Barcelona

Also popularly known as La Pedrera, «the stone quarry», it is one of the works in which Gaudí could advance most regarding his conception of ensemble and effective execution and which, accordingly, is a fine example of the degree of intensity that a genuine Gaudinian work can achieve, in spite of the fact that he did not finish it. This is something that happens in many of his works, e.g. the Sagrada Familia, the Güell Colony Church Crypt, Güell Park or the Episcopal Palace, whilst the Casa Batlló was a reform.

The Güell Wine Cellars
1895-1897/1903, Garraf

Here we can see typical elements of Gothic-style buildings, such as the loopholes over the entrance and the stone walls, which make this place look more like a castle than simple wine cellars, though somewhat «modernised». This was just before Charles Rennie Mackintosh undertook similar-looking works which also were reminiscent of Scottish fortresses. For both architects it was a way of seeking alternatives to the academicism of the time and of creating a national architecture.

Bellesguard
1900-1909/1916, Barcelona

Featuring a square ground-plan and situated in non-urban landscape, what in those days were the distant outskirts of Barcelona and with mediaeval-style elements such as the crenellation and the tower. The objectivity of working with pure geometry plus the subjectivity of recreating dreams of bygone days produce this splendid final result.

primitive Iberian stronghold to systematic Roman fortifications, and those which followed in order to guarantee the Arab Conquest and the Christian Reconquest. Far beyond those castles of stone, for centuries, the people of Catalonia have always aspired to construct much higher and more spectacular «buildings» with their own bodies. The origin of this unique tradition can perhaps be traced back to the way in which the Romans would storm walls. Groups of hundreds of people of all ages and sexes, the so-called *colles castelleres*, struggle to raise their members higher and higher, reaching amazing results of human towers of seven, eight, nine and even tiers. Without any doubt, this implies a knowledge, originally intuitive and popular, but now more and more scientific and technical, of the anatomy and the gravitational conditions for building with this original construction material. This all shows us a special sense of construction, ancestrally rooted in the people of Catalonia, to which the protagonist of this book proudly belonged. Antoni Gaudí i Cornet was born on 25th June, 1852 in Reus or in Riudoms (Tarragona), according to an old controversy regarding his exact place of birth. His figure is therefore shrouded in mystery since the day he was born, just like in legends, enveloped in that peculiar incertitude regarding the true origin of so many historical characters, which consequently makes them even more universal. However, whichever may be his exact cradle, something is clear: if Antoni Gaudí had died on 31st December,1899, he would not have been known to very many. And if he is famous all over the world today it is due to the work he carried out during the first quarter of the twentieth century until his death in Barcelona, on 10th June, 1926. This is said in order to claim him as an architect clearly belonging to the twentieth century.

If he were to be considered an architect belonging to the nineteenth century, then he would be classified (restrictively and wrongly) as a Modernist as opposed to modern, and not as the protomodern founder of modernity in his own right. And this is not just a gratuitous remark, as much has been said and written to this effect. In fact, there are many artists and architects included in chapters on the twentieth century who, indeed, died long before 1926.

So, without any antecedents in the family, and coming from five generations of coppersmiths, Gaudí decided to go to Barcelona to study architecture. He graduated as an architect in 1878 after somewhat irregular studies and a final exam which he passed with the minimum qualification. Meanwhile, his shortage of funds forced him to work as an assistant in several offices of local architects before being able to become independent with his own clientele.

Everything else in his life is linked to the development of his professional activity and works. He was greatly favoured when Eusebi Güell (1846-1918) discovered him in 1878. His acquaintanceship with this generous patron did not only lead him to creating works for him, but also to being commissioned by other members of high society; not very many, but enough to become an overwhelming milestone of architecture. With the result that a great number of books and information can be found in any library under the heading «Gaudí» . The only problem is that one must take care and critically interpret what one reads, due to the number of errors that have been published, not only regarding facts and chronologies, but even concerning the incorrect attribution of works to collaborators. And also due to the great number of gratuitous interpretations spread about his life and works which may be strictly and objectively refuted.

Güell Palace
1885-1888/1890, Barcelona
Detail of dome

Proof of Count Güell's admiration for Gaudi is that he entrusted him with works for himself. Here we have a view of the central main dome featuring a series of delicate holes as if they were an aureole of zenithal light. This space is designed in various heights which help to embellish its perception. It was destined to be used as an area for parties and concerts.

Güell Park
1900-1914, Barcelona

One of Gaudi's main works, due to Count Güell's patronage and his unprejudiced artistic sensibility, also thanks to which Antoni Gaudi has achieved world fame. Even in what had to be the simple infrastructure of a housing estate we can find crenellations and dragons, as well as a display of all those great concepts and minor details which make his works so extraordinary and intense.

13

Casa Vicens
1878-1880/1883-1888, Barcelona

It could well be said that this house was the first, his first serious professional assignment, as it is more complete than the previous ones and the best preserved to date. The rest have either been left only in the project stage or were built whilst Gaudí worked as an assistant to other architects, or are simply works of interior decorating or furniture designing: here, for the first time, he carries out every single detail designed for both the inside and the outside.

His Early Works

The beginning of an architect's practice is usually not a very easy one, and even more so with a social background such as Gaudí's, made even worse by the fact that he was not from the capital, but «from the provinces». This was not the best of situations for an architect who was about to start his career, meaning that he had to pave his own way. On the other hand, colleagues of his who had enjoyed a better start in life, not because they were more worthy of it or more skilled, but simply because they had been born into a well-to-do family, found things much easier. This had its immediate effects, since the difficulty of receiving commissions for projects as opposed to the easiness with which others got them, has brought as a result fewer and less important buildings. Something that has a «feedback» effect, as «money makes money», and completed works, new works.

Casa Vicens, Barcelona (1878-1880-), 1883-1888

A very cheerful, colourful and somewhat extravagant little house, which we could almost call a summerhouse. This is how we could describe Gaudí's first important commissioned project, which allows us to get an idea of its author's personality. It is full of intelligent architectural details that show us the affection and illusion of a young architect who had just graduated. Josep Francesc Ràfols comments in his book how he designed it between 1878 and 1880, meaning that he started to do so the very year in which he graduated. Although the plans were signed in 1883, this means its construction was carried out at the same time as his next building.

In order to give the *Casa Vicens* an airy effect, as if of an ephemeral construction, the outside of the building is covered in strongly contrasting green and white tiles, whose composition has almost textile connotations. This is complemented by a pattern of small yellow flowers and grilles in the shape of palmetto leaves, plants that apparently existed there on the site.

However, it is the meticulously-designed interior of the building that really reflects that idea of the project. The lavish plant motifs in the decoration of the spaces between the beams (in tiles and *papier mâché*) make the whole house look like a garden. The walls are concealed beneath paintings of flying birds and leaves, climbing ivy, stuccos and sgraffiti representing other plants on the upper floor. The walls and ceilings are in harmony thanks to the species of plants and colours chosen for their meaning, like the delicate shades of pink roses that appear in the main bedroom, symbols of love. The architect's love for detail can be also seen in the figure of a bird (originally two) that hangs from the ceiling

Casa Vicens
1878-1880/1883-1888, Barcelona

When Gaudí was going to start work on his first house, the Casa Vicens, *he felt sorry for the little yellow flowers that were on the construction site, so he decided to preserve them forever in tiles covering the whole building. The palmetto leaves that can be observed on the outer railings have the same origin. A magnificent example of somebody who respected the environment, long before anybody talked of ecology.*

Casa Vicens
1878-1880/1883-1888, Barcelona

Façades of rough stonework and geometrically-arranged tiles which turn into a chessboard-like white and green pattern as they go up and vertical lines that stylise and embellish the whole ensemble. Re-entrant and salient angles abound, as well as balconies and miradors, and elaborate chimneys, all reminiscent of Oriental forms of art.

in front of the chimney, in such a way that it moves when the hot air ascends. The woodwork on cupboards and doors is carried out to make them look like delicate screens. And we must not forget to highlight the creation of halls where the doors are, in the form of small wooden partitions leading into the various rooms.

Also the numerous intermediate spaces (some of which no longer exist), small balconies, galleries, lattices and trellises are part of the outside-inside continuity, the building being conceived as a recreational Mediterranean summerhouse; exactly the opposite of a solemn mansion in the strict academic tradition. The light of the Alhambra of Granada has triumphed over the shadows of the Greek or Roman Pantheon. And to make this more obvious, to make the most of and cover up the adjacent party wall, he embeds the building there, onto the very edge of the site.

The ensemble was finished off with a fountain, a belvedere and a mirador-waterfall with a grotto, which, unfortunately, today no longer exist as such since part of the site was sold, being reduced to the minimum and blocked off by some houses that have since been built. The house designed by Gaudí is now twice its original size, and, although the façades imitate the original ones, the inside of the building proves to be rather Classical and ordinary. Gaudí's original idea has clearly been distorted forever, something that he immediately intuited, which was why he refused to carry out any reforms.

Casa El Capricho, Comillas (Cantabria), 1883-1885

Meanwhile, hundreds of kilometres away, near Santander, work had begun on another little house. The distance, however, meant that Gaudí could not supervise the work with his usual meticulosity. Although he left it in the competent hands of his friend Cristóbal Cascante, it is evident that the final result is not up to the standards of other works by Gaudí.

There are numerous details similar to those of the *Casa Vicens*. For example, the same Oriental influence which Gaudí was so fond of, being especially attracted by the exoticism of far-off lands as he wished to seek alternatives to the academicist Classicism prevailing at the time. This explains the Indian-style tower, the Chinese-style gables over the balconies, or the Persian-style iridescent glazed tiles. In this sense, here he goes much further afield than Arabia, his dream for the *Casa Vicens*. However, other details are literally common: the same beautiful tiles with sunflowers, although in Barcelona not so profusely, to the extent that one may think that he has used up surplus material. The same occurs with the delicately bent vertical bars on the railings, or the horizontal rows of tiles on the façades, between the brickwork on *Casa El Capricho* and between the

El Capricho
1883-1885, Comillas

Just like in Casa Vicens, we have a decoration of horizontal bands of tiles which become more profuse as they ascend, with the purpose of lightening the upper part of the building. Here the balconies are even lighter than those seen in Casa Vicens, *being made entirely of iron in the way of Chinese-looking arbours. However, as usual in him, it is not merely a copy like his eclectic historicist contemporaries would make, but a very synthetical vague image.*

stonework on the *Casa Vicens*. There is also the similar idea of a little «summerhouse», and the garden and building understood as an ensemble, in this case not so well achieved. This is maybe deliberate, since the climate of the Cantabrian coast is quite different to that of the Mediterranean, and the greater separation between the interior and the exterior that can be seen in *El Capricho* would therefore be justified.

Both houses are built around a main central gallery facing south. And both have diagonal (45°) balconies and entrances, sometimes enhanced by vertical towers with small turrets, showing how Gaudí pays special attention to finishing off corners, using them to introduce peculiar, complex and contradictory elements. Many other similarities may be found, whether in the overall layout –for example the inside distribution– or in many other details: benches embedded into balcony railings, the balconies being on a lower level than the floor inside, grottos and water in their respective gardens, and the representation of birds and palmetto leaves.

An important novelty here is the way in which iron starts to take protagonism, which will be an essential component of his later works. Gaudí knew

El Capricho
1883-1885, Comillas

Amidst the rich foliage of the surrounding gardens, rises the slender little tower-mirador of the Marquis of Comillas' residence. It is covered with shimmering glazed green tiles which continue with the original Oriental fantasies of his first works, showing no interest in following the lines of the academicist Classicism, seeking alternatives to finding a modern architecture.

how to make the most of this material, showing us his skill and craftsmanship in its handling, achieving extremely original final results. Seemingly, this was sparked off by the belief that every house conceals a metaphor of music, a «caprice» in its meaning as a musical piece. This is why the whole building is covered in lines of the staff, represented in metal on railings and gables, crossed with free rhythmic curves left in the iron space, inspired by clefs and quavers. And, in the background, the singing of birds both inside and outside the house and the tinkling of the counterweights on the sash windows, as if they were real chords.

The Güell Stables, Barcelona, 1884-1887

The pavilions that make up the Güell Stables complete Gaudí's Oriental trilogy. Just like with the two previous houses, as soon as one sees them one is reminded of Oriental buildings.

Once again, because the overall image is one of a cheerful, intimate, airy and almost textile construction which is full of details. This time on a smaller scale, making the result more intimate, without imposing the monumentality of Classic architecture.

Together with this, its geometry, structure and colouring make us think of Arabesque architecture: the well designed brick ornamentation forming lattices, the walls covered in bold geometrical decoration or the use of coloured tiles. All this, made a lot easier because this work was carried out in Barcelona, with

The Güell Stables
1884-1887, ironwork, Barcelona
Dragon

This magnificent dragon is the most spectacular one of its kind in the History of Art and is a synthesis of all possible traditions: its sharp, pointed design reminds us of a dragon from the Far East; its subject matter refers to a dragon from Greek mythology; geographically-wise, it corresponds with a legendary Catalonian dragon; and, from a Christian and mediaeval point of view, it is the symbol of evil.

The Güell Stables
1884-1887, Barcelona

Today it houses the Càtedra Gaudí *(The Gaudí Chair), currently held by Juan Bassegoda who is in charge of the restoration and preservation of the buildings. From the very start of his career, Gaudí introduced his catenary-parabolic arch, something which had been used in Catalonian civil engineering since the 19th century, being considered the most stable type. With it, he justified those two main alternative sources to the* academicism *which years later would become generalised for building the new modern architecture. On the other hand, his geometrical and colourful treatment of brick and tiled latticework, as well as the ornamentation of the walls, give this building the impression of being a Moorish work. This Oriental idea is enhanced even more by the lanterns and air vents. However, once again it is important to point out that the different architectonic elements present here are not a copy of anything else; each detail is an entirely original one designed by Gaudí.*

Güell Palace
1885-1888/1890, Barcelona
Interior

Magnificent, almost Bizantine, interior, featuring rich ornamentation achieved through geometry and constructive ingeniousness, the main characteristics of what would later be modern architecture: it is the constructive detail itself which becomes the new modern ornament, free from the traditional Classical one. Here we can appreciate it in the rooms on the main floor, situated at the back of the house, where the architect also seeks to create smaller, more intimate, subspaces.

Güell Palace
1885-1888/1890, ironwork, Barcelona

Iron is an essential component of Gaudí's works, managing to make the most out of this material, by handling it in a simple, but ingenious manner, always in strict accordance with its characteristics. The results contrast greatly with the work of his contemporaries. Here we have a detail of one of his dragon-like serpents.

the almost constant presence of someone who liked to supervise his works very closely.

So, this conscious tendency towards Arab architecture has a lot to do with the search for a national architecture on the part of Gaudí and some of his colleagues. The nineteenth century was one of a special awakening of national consciousness, in Catalonia as well. Therefore, if architects from Northern Europe preferred Gothic art, Classic Greco-Roman art coming from the south, then Mudéjar or Mozarabic art had to be considered a more suitable model for Spain, since this was the only European country that had it. If in the two previous houses the protagonist was the ceramic tile, now it is clearly iron which takes over, with the spectacular appearance of the most famous wrought-iron dragon in the History of Architecture; of course, (as Juan Bassegoda states in his book *El Gran Gaudí*), with the symbolic background of wishing to recreate the Garden of Hesperides, belonging to Greek mythology (much loved by Count Güell) and appearing in the poem *L'Atlàntida* by Cinto Verdaguer (1845-1902), a mutual friend of the client and the architect of these buildings. With this literary excuse, the figure of the dragon finally appears in Gaudí's work. In this case, the dragon can be seen on the main gate like a fierce watchdog, mixing reality and legend, since it had to guard the golden fruit which Hercules sought. This is why it has such long claws and dangerous spikes all over its body; emerging from its threatening jaws full of teeth, a bifid tongue, designed and placed as if it had been originally meant as a handle for opening the gate. The estate could not have been made more secure, as only the dragon's nearest and dearest would dare to put their hand into the dragon's gaping jaws! And the shock would be even worse if the gate were to move at the same time as the claw. Of course, this never did happen, but, when we look carefully at the gate, at the position of the dragon, at the chains strategically placed in relation to the dragon (which also represent its mythological punishment and confinement), it is easy to think that this intention had in fact initially existed.

The Güell Palace, Barcelona, 1885-1888 (-1890)

With this building, his first major work, Gaudí's career as an architect took a new turn. Now it was not a case of building pretty summerhouses or pavilions, but something much more serious. It was the mansion, the city residence of a count (although he was not granted the title until 1910), the social image which he must give to the whole city (which is not a recondite or anecdotal fact). It was the public face of a nobleman, his banner, his castle. As a matter of fact, it was visited by many personalities, including Queen María Cristina of Spain, King Humbert of Italy and the US President Grover Cleveland.

This justifies the use of stone as the main material, which is now well cut, no longer rough rubblework, as opposed to the bricks and tiles (lighter and more popular materials) of his previous works. Now the traditional prestige of stone prevails. Strength, power and durability are the concepts which spring to one's mind on seeing it, which are just what was intended. And, along these lines, just like in any other palace, the coat of arms dominates the façade, featuring a helmet and a winged dragon «D'Aragó» (which is neither an eagle or a phoenix as some have said). In this case, it is that of Catalonia, but designed in iron in a very original way, since the four stripes of Catalonia can be

Güell Palace
1885-1888/1890, Barcelona
Chromatic detail

Light is another of the essential components of Gaudinian works, as well as being a resource for achieving chromatism. On the other hand, it is also a style of architecture that follows the maxims of authenticity of John Ruskin (1819-1900), which would also become part of the ethical principles of modernity: no building of false structures that do not have a supporting function; no placing of industrialised ornaments imitating artisan ones; or no simulation of materials as if they were other, more expensive ones.

perceived through the spiral coils on one bend. It is flanked by two wide catenary arches that are a splendid example of ironwork and the initials of its owner on some bars that remind us of those of *El Capricho*. And all this carried out in tune with the nature of the material, iron, but achieving its maximum expression, unknown until this moment.

The lively result achieved commands our attention and can be seen on many other metallic details on the inside. The catenary-parabolic arches inside and outside remind us of those at the Güell Stables. They are built in the form of a catenary, the curve formed by a hanging chain, which is the line of the natural way in which loads descend. At that time it was only used by Catalonian masons or engineers without any studies of History. Because this building has no echo whatsoever of historical styles, quite the opposite of what a learned and stylish architect of the times should build. There is no tripartite composition, no symmetry, no hierarchism, being free from the Classical language of architecture and its ornamentation like the rest of the house. Even when there are capitals they are invented like hyperboloids following nothing. As we can see, years before the

Güell Palace
1885-1888/1890, Barcelona

A plain façade, due to its bare functionality and neutral composition on the margin of orthodox Classical tradition. In any case, it is closer in spirit to the clearness, conciseness, constructivity and sincerity of Romanesque art: a style which would be adopted once again by architects such as Henry Hobson Richardson and the Chicago School as an alternative to Classicism.

Casa Tassel (1892-1893) by Victor Horta (1861-1947), made famous by historiographers of the Modernist movement, an unknown Antoni Gaudí was already preceding him in the non-historicist original design and the introduction of iron creating free forms in space.

But we cannot forget to highlight a number of even more surprising elements such as the following: the layout and distribution of spaces throughout the building; the mixed iron and wooden latticework; or the distribution of different chimneys featuring abstract geometric patterns on the flat roof, which are a culmination of the formal and colourist elements already introduced in his early roofs.

Works Outside Barcelona

Since the 1980s, and particularly during the nineties, Barcelona became definitively known to the whole world as «the city of Gaudí», a characteristic that attracts millions of visitors. This has to do with how and where he got the orders for his work, which meant a geographical concentration especially in Barcelona where the great majority of and the most important works are found.

However, the time came when he started receiving orders for works outside Barcelona, though not very many. Later would come the restoration of Palma de Mallorca Cathedral (1903-1914), and in La Pobla de Lillet, between 1905 and 1906, a small building and Artigas Gardens. And the odd significant project, like some Catholic missions in Tangier (1891-1893), a hotel in New York (1908) and a church in Rancagua (1922).

Episcopal Palace, Astorga (León), 1887-1893

A city that remembers its Roman origin with its well-preserved walls, next to which this palace was built. The work was also commissioned to Gaudí by a member of the nobility, but this time an ecclesiastical one, the Bishop of Astorga, partly with a similar concern for his public image, representativeness and solemnity. Like Gaudí's previous work carried out in stone (limestone from Garraf), once again this was to be the material chosen for building the Episcopal Palace (granite from El Bierzo), of a rougher texture and a sturdier aspect.

Other premises would be its location just next to the stone Cathedral of Astorga, of rosy warm tones, in contrast with the cold grey ones of the palace, as well as the fact that Gaudí was still struggling with the difficulties occasioned by the small site and extremely narrow street of the Güell Palace, wedged into a row of houses with very little outside space for working. It is logical that after the first projects which had offered him more freedom of volume, that of Güell Palace must have somewhat disheartened him, when he thought of all that he could not do because of so many pre-existing restrictions.

All of a sudden, he was being offered a project, an episcopal palace, with a completely free location, on an elevated site high above the old wall, without practically any restriction. Here Gaudí's unbounded imagination would be projected as far as the triumphal images of the European Neo-Gothic and Mediaevalist movement that he had been thinking about for years; a tendency that brought those fictitious times of heroes, romanticism and fairy tales nearer to us and made them come true. For example, the fairy-tale castle of *Neuschwanstein* («swan stone», in German) as if taken from a dream. Since his adolescent years

The Episcopal Palace
1887-1893, Astorga

With this building, which we can see towering high above the ancient Roman wall, Gaudí saw his opportunity to undertake projects outside Barcelona. First in Astorga and then in neighbouring León, precisely two cities of Roman origin. He had to travel more than 800 kilometres each way in order to direct the works, which was not very easy in those days, so he took advantage to deal with both works at the same time.

The Episcopal Palace
1887-1893, Astorga

In a similar way to what he would do, for example, in El Capricho, *he includes a protruding porch open on its four sides with magnificent arches intended as an area for welcoming the visitor. The large stone soffits making up the arches and the way they have been placed attract our attention, thus creating another curved subspace prior to the entrance.*

The Episcopal Palace
1887-1893, Astorga

It has been called the best Neo-Gothic building in the north of Spain. However, it would be better to say that more than a simple, faithful, ideal reproduction of the style characteristic of authentically Neo-Gothic architects, it is rather an original project that arises from the fascination towards a special period of heroes and legends –the Middle Ages- as an historical moment in which, furthermore, Catalonia was a world power.

even Gaudí would hear about the dreamlike castle that was being built in Southern Germany; ideals that can feed and determine the vocation of an architect. Or other more erudite or closer cases which he studied during his architecture studies, such as the French architect Eugène-Emmanuel Viollet-Le-Duc (1814-1879); influenced by his postulates, Gaudí set about not only recuperating an original Gothic style, but also surpassing it through new creation.

He began to understand that the Gothic style was an incomplete one which had to be brought to perfection. With this idea in mind, he took advantage of every moment and detail, making his building as vertical as possible, enhancing the folds and recesses on the façade, buttresses and corners, gable ends, chimneys, round towers (like the Roman ones on the edge of the site) etc. He also surrounded it with a moat, something more characteristic of a castle than an episcopal palace, although it also has its sanitary purpose of ventilating and giving light to the basement. The final result does indeed make us of think of North-

The Episcopal Palace
1887-1893, Astorga

*This building, seen here rising above the
Roman wall with its round stone towers,
right next to the Cathedral, is an
important part of the Astorga skyline,
standing out against the backdrop of the
Cantabrian Mountains. Its cold grey tone
contrasts with the warmer one of the
Cathedral, possibly emphasising its
interpretation from more oniric strata.*

European Mediaeval-Romantic castles, with high towers and princesses wearing
tall hats, the same shape as the conic roofs. However, it was not Gaudí who finished them off, falling out with the Diocesan Council after the death of his friend
and fellow countryman Bishop Joan Grau (1832-1893) who had entrusted him
with the project.

The Teresian School, Barcelona, 1888-1889

He also chose a battlemented castle for this project, with solid stone and brick
walls and sturdy corners. But this time austere in volume, of a simple rectan-
gular ground plan, no longer reflecting the image of noble wealth, but corresponding to conventual austerity since it was built for a religious congregation

The Teresian School
1888-1889, Barcelona

Once again, we have a building in the form of a castle with crenellation which does not belong to any style in particular and where the special stylisation of parabolic windows made it look even more mediaeval and enigmatical. At the same time, Gaudí, as usual, takes into account his clients' interests when designing his architectonic elements.

committed to frugality, the Order of St. Teresa, founded by St. Enric d'Ossó (1840-1896).

This project, together with the previous one, meant Gaudí was closer in contact with people of a profound spiritual life who were particularly concerned about spreading Catholicism. Therefore, it was the culmination of his contacts with three other key ecclesiastical figures with whom he had been dealing for years: Josep María Bocabella (1815-1892), founder of the *Asociación de Devotos de San José*, the promoter of the construction of the *Sagrada Família*, Gaudí taking over its works in 1883 and his friends Cinto Verdaguer, the priest, and Josep Torras (1846-1916), the bishop. Obviously, the simultaneous contact with var-

The Teresian School
1888-1889, Barcelona

The horizontal rows of bricks alternating with rubblework (less expensive than regular dressed stone) on the façades come from popular architecture, and favour the sturdiness of the walls as they go up. Both these horizontal bands and the upper storey built totally of ceramic bricks, facilitate the binding of the walls and, therefore, the solidity of the whole building.

ious saints of the Catholic Church must have had a deep influence on him, his existential outlook changing forever. From that moment on, his works would reflect his need to express his religious belief and feeling. And, if his early works hardly contain any symbols of Christianity, now the latter would be incorporated in the most prominent places of his buildings.

To start with, in this building we see for the first time how he places his characteristic four-armed cross, which he would include in later works, as a final mark of offering his works to God. This idea occurred to him just in time to hastily place a simple Greek cross, still bidimensional, on the highest part of the Güell Palace. However, in the Teresian School, he had more time to elaborate the theme, and, as he raised the corners in pinnacles, he decided to finish them off in the same style as Gothic cathedrals, with four-armed cross shapes. The rest of the symbology can be found between the grilles, in the form of inscriptions, mortarboards (it is a school and St. Teresa is a Doctor of the Catholic Church) and Teresian coats of arms on the corners and on the main entrance.

The latter has an iron gate which synthesises the lines of those coats of arms in metal: Mount Carmel crowned with a cross and a star in the middle, flanked by the hearts of St. Teresa (pierced by the arrow of her transfixion) and the Virgin Mary (wounded by the crown of thorns). On the grilles of the ground floor windows, the anagram of Jesus Christ alternates with a subtle representation of the flames of divine love, achieved through a coherent and simple tectonicity of iron. Meanwhile, the inside is made up of longitudinal rooms arranged along the façades and a central part consisting of corridors around large inner courtyards full of light. The light is reflected on the parabolic arches that result in a

typically Gaudinian space, diaphragmed and rhythmic, which we first saw at the Güell Stables.

Casa Fernández y Andrés (Casa Botines). León, 1891-1892

Located in a square in the centre of a capital city as old as Spain, this house is surrounded by historical mediaeval vestiges and, like in Astorga, is next to the Roman wall dating from the times of the Seventh Le(gi)on, which gave León its name. These circumstances justify the use of stone for building this house which is known as the *Casa Botines* or *Casa Fernández y Andrés*, the surnames of its two

owners. Their business had been formerly established by Joan Homs Botinàs, from where the popular name of *Botines* comes.

The house is finished with roughly dressed stone, making it look more rustic and old. But the ground plan is freed from traditional carrying walls (except, for reasons of economy, on the upper floors), being replaced by a structure of simple, slender cast iron pillars. Without any historicist concern, he leaves them uncovered, not worrying about their functional bareness or bothering about any Classicist recreation, when, being faced with such a new building material, the normal thing would be to decorate the tops of the metal pillars with ridiculous pseudo-Corinthian iron motifs. This was usually done because they were not too sure about which were the «right» forms for the new proportions allowed by iron, and is why they resorted to the only defined architectonic language, the Classic one, although it applied to works made of stone and not iron.

The free ground-plan achieved here by Antoni Gaudí is no more than the culmination of previous works since he received his first major commission, the project for the Güell Palace, following a structure of summers and pillars: the latter built mainly of stone, as this way they look less industrial and more no-

Casa Botines
1891-1892, León

The trefoil-style arches on the windows that we can see here also appear on the façade of the Episcopal Palace, but signs of them can also be observed on Casa Vicens. The main entrance is a flatter version, though a heptafoil one, of the soffits over the entrance of the Episcopal Palace. Above, the stone statue of St. George slaying the dragon, and inside the same arch, a metallic lion similar to the dragon on Güell Palace.

33

ble, in accordance with the use of the building as a palace. And, at the same time as he was building the Episcopal Palace in nearby Astorga, he gave the *Casa Botines* a similar aspect, although somewhat simpler and not so lordly, but which equally evokes a mediaeval castle. For example, just like his building in Astorga, not only is it surrounded by a moat, which is more befitting of a castle than a commercial building and houses, but its corners are also enhanced with round pointed towers. Right on the corners, the points which have to be the most reinforced ones of the building, and which are, in military architecture, the most efficient for defence, since it is from protruding corner towers that the two façades can be controlled and the next towers sighted. Besides this, corners are also the part to which Gaudí pays particular attention, treating them in an especially complex manner, throughout all his career starting from the *Casa Vicens*. This was a subject corroborated by the treatment of the corner on the *Palacio de los Guzmanes* standing opposite, a detail that frequently appears in Spanish historical architecture, especially in Renaissance civil architecture. In fact, this corner is different to the other three. Lastly, the main entrance is protected by a stone statue of St. George slaying the dragon over and above a lion made of wrought iron, completely surrounded by characteristic ironwork, in this case a dangerously spiky one. We could say, with the same defensive purpose as Count Güell's palace and stables.

The Güell Wine Cellars, Garraf (Barcelona), 1895-1897 (-1903)

Gaudí's works can also be found in the province of Barcelona outside the capital city. In this case, in the form of cellars for his patron, Count Güell, on part of his wild land located on the cliffs of Garraf overlooking the Mediterranean Sea. Therefore, this time, we do not have the more or less consolidated urban context which Gaudí was used to. In this case, the only remarkable neighbour-

The Güell Wine Cellars
1895-1897/1903, Garraf

With the appearance of a Viking stone ceremonial building or vessel, as if coming from some distant or prehistoric culture, related to the most genesiac of the human act of building, and free from any historical style, stands this construction overlooking the sea. Its artificer was sensitive enough to open up a sheltered terrace-cavern in the prow facing the sea. With its original chimneys and the «G» for Güell on the front drawn just as lightly as his first «G» for Gaudí on his own desk or the one at the Güell Stables.

ing buildings are not much more than the ruins of an old mediaeval watchtower, a construction which is frequently found along the coast, erected to defend it from Moorish pirate raids.

Once again, he chose stone, connected with the existing ancient fortification, here the mediaeval forms being even more stylised, with towers, strongly-defended gates with aggressive iron claws, battlements and loopholes. However, in spite of featuring all these elements, the popular image of the commonplace castle is not evoked as directly as occurs in Gaudí's creations in Astorga and León; instead, we could say that here it is his intention to surpass it. It is more like an attempt to evoke the same image between romantic and magical, but, instead of doing so from an imaginative look to the past, it is designed projected towards contemporaneity. And so, it boldly faces the infinite sea horizon, with a pointed façade as if it were a defiant prow of a ship. In fact, at its head, there is a mirador facing the sea, almost as if it were the bridge of an enormous ship. After all, it must have been from these cellars that the wine served at the tables of the *Compañía Transatlántica* ships came, the company which belonged to Antonio López (1817-1883), Marquis of Comillas and Count Güell's father-in-law.

Something was beginning to change in Gaudí's architecture. When he found himself there, all alone, face to face with nature and its uncontrollable forces, far away from any architectural reference, and without any human conventions, his personal and creative historical figurativism initiated an important process of transformation, towards a much greater and more sublime power of fascination. In fact, this had always been a part of him, since, when he was a child, he would stop to contemplate the *Campo de Tarragona,* his home region. However, his studies of architecture managed to veil this.

The Güell Wine Cellars
1895-1897/1903, Garraf

The characteristic catenary-parabolic arches appear once again, in brick, stone and iron, as the gate of iron chains hangs freely. At the end of its great diagonal bar we immediately make out the body, claws and jaws of a stylised dragon. The gate is the evolution towards the abstraction of the one at Güell Stables, also made up of hanging chains.

On the other hand, these cellars have been one of his most controversial projects, to the extent that, due to an innocent historiographical error on the part of some, or to the obscure interest of others, it has either not been quoted as a Gaudinian work, or attributed to Francesc Berenguer (1866-1914), one of Gaudí's collaborators. The more ill-intentioned use the tactic of giving the glory to the disciples, thus taking away the authorship of the master in order to detract merit from him; instead of proceeding in a more honourable way, admitting that the planets are only visible when illuminated by the sun. However, there is no need to carry on with such comments due to the extensive literature available on the subject which Juan Bassegoda provides in his book. Besides, anybody who has a minimum idea of spaciality and architecture, as well as of its details, but especially of basic architectonic concepts, can see that this work fits in perfectly with the Gaudinian evolution. If it were to be attributed to Francesc Berenguer alone (except for some elements which are easily recognisable), it would turn out to be a strange, isolated work.

Güell Park
1900-1914, Barcelona
Pavilion roof section

One of the pavilions at the entrance, with its crenellation and parapets in the form of a round tower protecting the entrance, but now undulating with totally organic and unitary forms inspired on lichens and fungi. The lively chromatism is obtained by means of the trencadís *technique, taking advantage of waste material found, long before the terms «sustainability» or «Povera Art» were coined. Antecedents to this Gaudinian tendency of using nature as the model and abstraction as the method can be found in the Casa Calvet. And he achieved all this in the middle of his professional career, after a quarter of a century's work, with another quarter still to go.*

The Turn of the Century, the Start of a Definitive Rupture

Halfway through the 19th century, the idea that the modern day lifestyle in a period of increasing industrialisation had nothing to do with that of the past spread from Great Britain all over Europe. Therefore, as each period has to have its style, the question was which was the style of the modern period, the «modern style». Towards the end of the century, this feeling increased in the fields of art and culture. «The old» was coming to an end and something «new» had to found, anything. Everything was permitted, the unknown and the novel being highly valued just for that very reason. So, when the movement which at that time pursued «the modern», Modernism, finally came upon a new artistic language that seemed a systematic one, an *art nouveau* («new art»), it greeted it effusively.

Such was the climate surrounding Gaudí as well at the turn of the century, whilst his work was heading towards a definitive rupture with a Classical-Historicist tradition which he had, in fact, not followed very much, absorbed by his work from the very beginning, freely building in accordance with the times, precisely the characteristics of a new modern tradition.

Casa Calvet, Barcelona, 1898-1899

This is the evidence of the definitive turn taken by Gaudí in his career as an architect towards the end of the century, after two decades of evolution. He began the house looking unconsciously towards the past, as if out the corner of his eye, and finished it (obvious in final details and furniture) looking solely towards the future. There is a definitive rupture between before and after, finally breaking loose from the past and heading into the future with fully modern architecture, at the same time visionary and precursory, without any hindrance coming from Classical tradition.

This occurred when he was 46 years old: it is said that one does not become a true architect until well into one's forties. Ludwig Mies van der Rohe (1886-1969) was 43 when he designed the German Pavilion in Barcelona. Until then he had not built anything special (apart from four drafts for the same number of projects), and, if he had not carried on, he would have been consigned to oblivion. And today he is considered to be one of the great modern figures of architecture.

In order to illustrate this superposition of Gaudí's two tendencies in the *Casa Calvet*, as to the first one, we could point out the general symmetrical composition that is over-adorned both on the inside and outside, with certain Baroque reminiscences, wreathed columns, curves of a simple geometry on gables and balconies, cornucopias and garlands, and the stone façade finished off in a Roman style. However, the second one is now a vision of the future of his work, appearing on the upper balconies, part of the oriel, handles, knobs, peepholes, certain particular finishes and, surprisingly, in some furniture. There, his historical memory having now become exhausted, his creation would be fed from working with the material itself, its characteristics, possibilities and processes. The result would be a unique formal renovation.

In spite of everything, religious symbols and homages to the owners would still appear. From the doorknocker in the shape of a cross on the door over an insect representing evil, to a couple of crosses on the top, saints' busts with the palms of their martyrdom. For example, those of St. Giles of Arles and St. Giles of Rome, patron saints of Vilassar, the hometown of the Calvet family. Or St. Peter, because of the name of the head of the family which was also that of the textile firm. All this, turned into the source of new symbols, both in the house and its furniture, making constant references to hanks, reels belonging to the textile industry, thread and rope, whether in stone, wood or iron.

On the other hand, the *Casa Calvet* features a series of peculiarities and paradoxes that are worth mentioning. To begin with, it is his most conventional-looking building, and it is the only one for which he received an official award (maybe for that reason). With the added honour that he was the first person to be awarded the Barcelona City Council's architecture prize, which had recently been established in 1899. However, this did not mean that he would later be granted any important public project. The prize had been awarded to a house that had started being built without the corresponding permit: even the order was given at one stage to stop the works. And to make matters worse, it did not comply with the maximum height permitted by the city council. This had been previously pointed out on the plans, but Gaudí decided to go ahead with his project, reaching the height he considered appropriate, more than the one legally permitted. In spite of everything, no passer-by who is not an expert is able to spot this, since this house passes unnoticed within the new area of expansion (*l'Eixample*) of Barcelona, full of similar buildings. However, no prizes would be received for his following buildings, those that would give him world fame.

Güell Colony Church, Santa Coloma de Cervelló (Barcelona), (1898-) 1908-1917

This is one of his five key works: the 20th century is about to begin and, with it, Gaudí starts work on those building that would make him immortal. Now then, what «style» does this building belong to? Certainly not to *Art Nouveau* if we take this as a «style». Maybe to the «tectonic» style, if we might invent such a term. It only resembles itself, only with regard to its pure construction and structure, and to the immanence of the architecture, it does not look like anything outside its own materiality and objectivity, nor does it follow any arbitrary formalist or abstract model.

And it is in the microcosm that he creates with this building where symbols and connections with an intangible sphere prevail. In relation with our origin, since the most ancient of Christian symbols appear: alphas and omegas, the first and last of the Greek letters, symbols of Jesus Christ insofar as God is said to be the beginning and the end of all things. Fish, represented in an ingenuous

Güell Colony Church
1898-1908-1917, Barcelona
Outside view of the crypt

This lower, semi-underground section is the only part completed of what was originally intended to be a whole church. Its windows makes one think in a Surrealist way of latent eyes opening up in the walls. His treatment of the walls, both on the inside and outside, anticipates in architecture what many years later would be known as Brutalism and Informalism in art.

way, next to a display of fishing nets which are, in fact, the window grilles, in memory of the Apostles, and as Eucharistic symbols of the miracle of the multiplication of the bread and the fish appearing in the Gospel. Crosses of a *Via Crucis* with its 14 stations, a penitent approach to the holy ground. And this in the porch of the entrance to the crypt and the grotto under the staircase going up to what would have been the main floor if work on the church had not come to a halt.

On the entrance, we have the representation of a compendium of Catholic doctrine on one panel: the three Theological Virtues (Faith, Hope and Charity), presided over by the cross and flames of Charity as the most important; in between, the four Cardinal Virtues (Justice, Prudence, Temperance and Fortitude); on the sides, ears of wheat and bunches of grapes, symbols of the Eucharist (as the most sublime sacrament, it would represent the other six), fruit (recalling the twelve fruits of the Holy Ghost), palm leaves and olive branches corresponding to the triumphal entrance of Jesus Christ into Jerusalem, and symbols and anagrams representing the Trinity of Heaven and Trinity of Earth.

In order to achieve this, he did something that is unique in the History of Christian Art: he subtly fuses their respective anagrams, casting one on top of the other: F-SSS-P (*Filius-SpirituSanctuS-Pater*) and IHS-M-IHP (*Iesus-Maria-Ioseph*). The last three had already been used on the *Casa Batlló*. On the left, we have the *I*, for *Iesus* and *Ioseph*: which turns into the *F* for *Filius* (Son). In the centre, he places the two *H*'s with the *M* for *Maria*: which becomes the *SSS* for *SpirituSanctuS* (Holy Ghost). All this in the centre like the union and fruit of Father and Son. Just like Mary as the intercessor between God (Jesus) and man (Joseph). On the right, the *P* for *Pater* (Father) and *Ioseph*, which is also the *S* for *Iesus*. The final result is a synthesis achieved by graphical and conceptual su-

Güell Colony Church
1898-1908-1917, Barcelona
Staircase

If anybody were to think that his forms are arbitrary ones, they would only be showing their ignorance of the reasons that guided Gaudí. For instance, the case of this winding irregular-shaped flight of stairs leading up to what was going to be the main floor. In order to build it more easily it would have been necessary to fell a large pine tree that was standing on the site. However, Gaudí preferred to leave it where it was: after all, a tree takes a lot longer to grow than a staircase to make. But one day the age-old pine tree disappeared, nothing took its place and the staircase was left there looking rather odd. This shows us how respectful he was towards nature and the environment in an age when nobody talked of ecology like today.

Güell Colony Church
1898-1908-1917, Barcelona
Inside view of the crypt

Although obviously much lower, here we can get a pretty good idea of what the church might have looked like if it had been completed. The slanting, Brutalist-style pillars and the brick ribbed vault follow the corresponding catenaries on the natural load of the upper weights. An overall effect of primitive architecture is created which impresses us with its genesiac tectonicity.

perposition, a metaphor of the same way of spiritual identification of the Christian with Jesus Christ, who, as God and Man, belongs to both Trinities.

Another synthetic symbol, repeated on a lesser scale, appears on the ceiling: this time, a saw above an *M* (for *Maria* and an outline of mountains), which is, at the same time, the carpenter's saw («*sierra*» in Spanish) of St. Joseph and the *Sierra* (mountain range) of Montserrat («*monte serrado*», literally meaning «serrated mountain»), for which a scene of a monumental Rosary (1900-1916) had also been designed, even including the *I-M-I* for *Iesus-Maria-Ioseph*.

In fact, these symbolic mosaics were a minor rehearsal for what he was planning at that time, but on a larger scale, for the *Sagrada Familia*. Just like the whole architectural structure, for which he had made a scale model, hanging strings and weights to scale, in order to assess the respective pressure that would have to be supported. He took a photograph and turned the picture upside down, thus being able to visualise the angle that the slanting pillars should have, the exact shapes of the arches, vaults and domes, because the hanging cables follow the line of the natural load of the ceiling: it is a case of throwing catenaries into space, something that he had applied bidimensionally in his works from the beginning. And so he began to construct the slanting pillars of the crypt, exactly opposed in the same direction of the respective pressure; therefore, with the minimum of materials he could achieve the ideal structural work. There is nothing arbitrary in the forms. If anybody thinks otherwise, then they would only be showing their ignorance of the reasons that guided Gaudí.

Güell Park, Barcelona, 1900-1914

Another one of Gaudí's key works and his only town planning project. It comprises the necessary land development for the later sale of allotments where 60 houses surrounded by gardens were to be built, providing housing for 300 people; in fact, it was intended as a suburb, with its own streets, main square, market and even a chapel, although it never did get built. It was to be surrounded by a wall for security purposes and the main entrance gate, like in the Güell Stables, was flanked on either side by two pavilions: the porter's lodge and an office building. The *plaza,* an open public meeting place, also designed as a covered place where people could meet, which was also going to be the housing estate's marketplace.

As reveals its name, it was another of the initiatives promoted by Eusebi Güell. But, due to the failure in their commercialisation, the houses were not even built; neither did the fact that both the count and Gaudí decided to live there help. But the work that was carried out is more than enough to reveal Gaudí's ideal concept of town planning. To begin with, the title that he gave to the ensemble and inscribed along the whole perimeter wall is extremely illustrative: the words «Park Güell», spelt with a «k» like in English, whilst in Catalan it is spelt with a «c». This detail and the overall idea projected makes one think that he had been inspired by the recently invented English garden-cities, which were lately becoming more and more widespread, starting to appear on the Continent. Without any doubt, in this case, it was intended for a public with a certain standard of living. It also contrasted with the ideas of cities of the future that were frequent at the time. From the «Industrial Town» (1901-1904) of the French architect Tony Garnier (1869-1948), to the «New Town» (1914) of the Italian architect Antonio Sant' Elia (1888-1916), already manifestly vertical, influenced by the representation of the city of the future that was coming to Europe, due to the impact caused by the image of American skyscrapers at the beginning of the twentieth century.

All this had nothing to do with the concept of town planning proposed by Gaudí, of radically excelling a conventional implementation in nature, however

Güell Park
1900-1914, Barcelona

On the one hand, the whole park seems to be an original repertoire of solutions to the technical problems faced when having to build a retaining wall. On the other, Gaudí undertakes an architectonic-development project which goes much further than the 19th-century idea of a garden-city, anticipating in almost one century the current conception of fitting a traditional architectural work into its surroundings, to the extent that the dichotomy must disappear, in order to introduce the idea that it is actually a matter of creating the environment itself.

Güell Park
1900-1914, Barcelona

A common covered space, whose style may at first seem Greco-Roman but which looks like something out of dream anticipating Surrealism, where ceilings undulate like sheets blowing in the wind, architraves look broken, columns slant and capitals seem to melt and *sink into their shafts. Here the stone of the columns and Doric capitals, which are precisely the expression of maximum sturdiness, appear with characteristics that are not theirs. And, by means of* objets trouvés *and* collage-assemblage *on ceilings and benches we can also say that here we have an antecedent of Dadaism and all the movements that were to use such avant-garde techniques.*

respectful it may be, knowing that this respect is guaranteed in his case. With the result that, on one hand, he built with stone found on the actual site and, on the other, the roads, streets and paths fit in naturally with the terrain, to the extent that the hillside is left untouched. Refusing to disturb nature with levelling processes, he preferred to carefully integrate the streets of the complex in the form of viaducts. By using the latter he achieves such an integrated and tectonic effect that the final result goes much further than the simple use of nature as a mere background; Gaudí manages to blend form and substance as he works «with» nature, not «in» nature: or should we say, he designs the landscape itself, nature itself.

This concept can clearly be seen in the series of retaining walls built throughout the park which fit in with the viaducts, a splendid example of the constructive intelligence and creativity of this architect. Some of them incorporate the slanting columns that support the upper pressures and direct them towards the ground, just like in the Güell Colony Church. His use of large plantpots, just like at *El Capricho*, helps to verticalize the loads, as if they were rough natural pinnacles, with their same structural function as in the Gothic.

Meanwhile, a series of large stone balls were placed on the verges of all the roads, as if they were a Rosary on a huge scale, culminating in a string of Marian ejaculations (of which very few are left due to unfortunate restorations) inscribed on the famous undulating, ergonomic bench in the square. The words referring to the Virgin Mary as the «road of peace» are repeated several times, that in her hand, life is a road of peace toward the Far Beyond – a metaphor of the roads in the park, hoping that, by placing them under the protection of the Rosary, they will be filled with peace, the same road of prayer, of peace. On the other hand, it is in such an insignificant detail as those balls of stone where Gaudí's mastership can be seen, in something that is so important for architecture as the scale of things. If they had been made just a little bit bigger or smaller, then they would not have been of any use at all, since they are just the right size for sitting comfortably on, standing on to scan the horizon, jumping over or even for being tenderly embraced!

Casa Figueras (Bellesguard), Barcelona, 1900-1909 (-1916)

The very location of this manor house was an excuse to build once more evoking Gothic-mediaeval castles, since this was once the site of a residence belonging to King Martí, known as «the humane one» (1356-1410). Its name, *Bellesguard*, means «beautiful view» in Catalan, and is due to the site being on a hill overlooking the city. Its remains are still tangible, having been reconstructed, and their presence gives the place a specially Romantic atmosphere.

The building is a pure cube, which merges extremely well into the landscape, with the same heavy-set look of a castle. Its stone walls with narrow Gothic-style windows are also crowned with battlements and a «parapet walk», more characteristic of a fortress, although the crenellations are not so organic or colourful as those in Güell Park. And, also like in Güell Park, once again, a pointed tower crowns his work with a cross on the top. Each of its arms point to each of the four cardinal points and towards the sky, in a cosmological and metaphysical position, it harmonises the material and the spiritual. This cross represents, at the same time, both a physical and spiritual reference point: a compass card and the cross of Christ placed there as a guiding light.

And below, the crown alluding to the mediaeval king that ruled the lands of the Crown of Aragón from here, represented further down by the four red and yellow Catalano-Aragonese stripes. In this way, in a vertical hierarchical order,

Bellesguard
1900-1909/1916, Barcelona

An example of the way Gaudí relates the spiritual to the material is observing how the Christian crosses which crown his buildings are at the same time compass cards, cosmological signs that join them to the four cardinal points. This tendency can be seen on the Casa Vicens, *where words alluding to the direction of the sun can be observed on each façade and will be magnified in the* Sagrada Familia.

he placed the symbols of the King of the Cosmos and the King of Catalonia. The four stripes are coiled helicoidally like in the coat of arms at Count Güell's palace; spirals and helicoids, lines and surfaces much to his taste, which he used more and more frequently in his buildings. They already appeared on the axis of the gate of the Güell Stables, in details and on the chimneys of the Güell Palace, on some inside columns and on the corners of the Teresian School, on other columns of the *Casa Calvet*, in Güell Park, and even doubly, in opposite directions, on his high pinnacle: similar to what he imagined for the pillars of the *Sagrada Familia*, which also incorporates those forms in other places. He includes them in all the materials that he works with, in any detail, with all their

symbolic meaning, knowing that they express the upward movement much better than a simple vertical, corroborated by nature in tree trunks and plant stalks.

It can be seen how his architecture is, above all, one of synthesis like no other. The human and the divine blend together with the same organicity of nature. And the physicity of his works shows the perfect union between construction and space. Everything blends in with its surroundings, with the movement of whole volumes or with odd elements, such as the crenellations or embedded stones, especially present in Güell Park, which blend the building in with its background; the container and the contents, whether belonging to the material world or to the spiritual one and also between themselves, always delicately related and in union. This is why his disciple Josep Francesc Ràfols, in his book *Gaudí: 1852-1926*, says: «The reason that some Catalonian architects have understood him better than others is not because they are more prepared than the others from a technical point of view, (…) since Gaudí, seen from outside Faith, will always be incomprehensible. Maybe the incredulous will admire an aspect of his work, but not its synthesis.»

Bellesguard
1900-1909/1916, Barcelona

In this picture several recurrent themes in Gaudí's work can be highlighted. On the one hand, the different treatment of the top floor or upper perimetral gallery. Then we have the outline of sharp crenellations designed to contrast with the sky. Finally, the use of techniques such as the trencadís, *made up of small roughly-cut stones.*

The Prime of the Genius

Gaudí has now definitively left Classic tradition and its architectonic language far behind. Now he fully takes part in the birth of the new modern tendency being created all over by the most advanced architects. Some of the first complete and brilliant phrases in history to do with this new architectural language are his, in which everything was still to be done. And with those «phrases», with those works, after quarter of a century, Gaudí reaches his prime. At last, it results in an oasis of immense freedom, where each one of his projects is a world-famous architectonic milestone; even though he always had shown his enormous constructive-structural creativeness and genius, his extraordinary plasticity in these utterly new inventions with so much character, right from the very start, especially if we compare his buildings with the context of their time.

Casa Batlló («Casa dels Ossos»: «House of the Bones») Barcelona, 1904-1906

It is not surprising that, when it was being built, people started to call this house the «House of the Bones», though this is not such a well-known name nowadays. The entire façade looks as if it is covered with bones, skulls, shoulder blades or hip bones, in the form of bone-coloured balconies, as well as real visions of shinbones and fibulas on the lower part. (Balconies that began to gestate their strange metallic shapes since the design of the upper balconies of the *Casa Calvet*.) All this, together with a little round turret on the top which is crowned with the four-armed cross, and its singular roof which looks like a dragon's back, with its perfectly defined scales, make one immediately think of something which falls in line with Gaudí's inner world: a huge sword of Saint George, with the anagrams of Jesus, Joseph and Mary, has been thrust into the dragon's belly, and is surrounded by the bones of its victims lying at its feet.

On the other hand, Salvador Dalí (1904-1989) would be delighted at this house, as would any other lover of Surrealism, since it fitted in ideally with his ideal of «edible» architecture, of melted cheese or a runny omelette slithering slowly onto passers-by; all that fascinated him, applicable to his personal vision of the *Casa Batlló*. Absolutely nothing to do with the natural properties of stone with which the house has been built, a technique that Surrealism would make its own as a source and as a creative system. In fact, many are the times that

Casa Milà
1906-1910/1911, Barcelona
Chimney pots

Here, up on the rooftop, we have a whole landscape of complex, abstract, geometrical shapes, which twist and turn endlessly. Gaudí makes a mountain out of a house; a landscape out of a rooftop. Completed about twenty years earlier, the rooftop of Güell Palace already showed signs of this abstraction, though in a simpler, more linear manner. If we compare both we can see how they have evolved.

Casa Batlló
1904-1906, Barcelona
Balconies

The brightly-coloured glazed tiles covering the whole house are in line with the Macropointillism with which Henri Matisse was commencing the Fauvist movement during the same period. Whereas the inspiration for the trefoil-shaped balconies with iron railings can be traced back to the Casa Calvet.

Casa Batlló
1904-1906, Barcelona

Gaudí's respect for nature leads him to respecting the urban landscape, as we can see here, where he does away with the upper left-hand side of the façade in order to fit it in with the neighbouring Casa Ametller. *However, the same cannot be said for the architect and/or the promoter of the house on the right, since they speculatively raised it a further two storeys, leaving the side detail of the* Casa Batlló *meaningless.*

Dalí represents flesh held up by thin stick-like supports (crutches) in a very similar way to what can be seen here on this façade.

However, it is clear that the endless interpretations of the shapes, forms and colours of Gaudí's works are simply caused by their suggestive organicity and chromatism, which make us believe we are seeing something specific; just like when we imagine figures in the clouds, in ink stains or in streaks of marble etc.

Along these lines, many different things have been said: that it is the representation of the Venice Carnivals, with masks, confetti and array of colours; that it the image of a «vertically-constructed» lake, with its watery reflections, water plants and underwater caves; that it is the recreation of autumn skies and leaves blowing over Montserrat, the sacred mountain of Catalonia. However, it does not represent anything in particular, except abstract shapes and forms designed just for their own sake, in a coherent interaction with their constructivity. This work was conceived by Gaudí alone, directly giving orders, like a conductor, to the workmen who were on the scaffolding, telling them exactly where to put each coloured piece. Nobody else took part in its conception as some have tried to prove on more than one occasion. Rather, we could say that he was the antecedent, in architecture, to the Abstract Expressionism of artists such as Vasilii Kandinsky (1866-1944) or Jackson Pollock (1912-1956).

Artigas Gardens, La Pobla de Lillet (Barcelona), 1905.

Situated amidst lush landscape in the north of Catalonia near the Pyrenees, is a small workers' settlement which still partly conserves the taste of the beginning of the period of industrialisation. Here, at the beginning of the 20th century, Gaudí was commissioned the design of recreational gardens for the owner's family and acquaintances, next to his textile factory; somewhere to stroll, picnic, talk about business, close a deal in pleasant surroundings, also in line with the concern for a good public image. All this was very much connected with the expansion of Modernism in Catalonia at the turn of the century.

Gaudí, once again, fits these gardens into their natural surroundings in the most delicate and natural way. Or, at least, this is what it seems, because, what he in fact did was recreate the landscape itself. Just like in Güell Park, which is also very similar in various aspects, also using the materials found in the area. Stones are piled up naturally to form arches or disappear into grottos; they hang or protrude, breaking simple, straight lines, and, instead, form a complex, uneven line, which is in accord with nature. Half-embedding stones into the silhouettes of his works, letting them stand out from their sharp outline, half in, half out, in Güell Park, *Bellesguard*, the *Sagrada Familia* … which all contribute to the certain magical atmosphere of these gardens.

And, if water flows out of a dragon's mouth in a fountain at Güell Park, here it flows from a lion and a bull. These animals are also placed like a virtual cross together with an eagle near the tower-mirador and a winged human figure or an angel (now gone) on another high fountain. They are the four figures of the Christian Tetramorphs, which appear in apocalyptic iconography escorting Jesus on his second coming at the end of the world. It was a favourite subject of those days, not only his, and he would put it in a privileged place of the *Sagrada Familia*. For example, Lluís Domènech represents it in the pavilions of Santa Creu

Artigas Gardens
1905, La Pobla de Lillet

Stones, laid with the same trencadís *technique used for placing his ceramic tile fragments, are arranged here in a helicoidal manner. This time creating only symbolically functioning elements, as a Surrealist would say. But this helicoidal form appears practically in all his works from the very beginning, especially in all kinds of pillars: it could be said that it is the subjective manifestation of his own will of elevation, a life guided by ideals and the objective expression of movement.*

i Sant Pau Hospital that he was building at that time (1901-1912). Also connected with this, on the upper part, Gaudí created a kind of a long trumpets of the Last Judgement coiled around each other, continuing with his beloved helicoids. Other interpretations could be evil reptiles, snakes, or strange oneiric mushrooms, of undulating, rhythmic movements, like those on the roof of the *Casa Batlló*.

Meanwhile, the River Llobregat, flows along in a lively manner below, the river which 135 km further south supplies the city of Barcelona with water. In short, it is a work carried out with great ingenuousness, as usual, giving it its characteristic freshness and candidness, built by someone who takes what he is doing very much to heart. Something that fascinated the artists of historical vanguards, when they came closer to the naïve art of children to learn from spirits that have not been corrupted by conventions or academic malformations. This is Gaudí, with his delightful utopian romanticism, but with his constructive sincerity; at the same time, with his head in the clouds, but with his feet firmly on the ground.

Casa Milà («La Pedrera»: «The Stone Quarry»), Barcelona, 1906-1910 (-1911)

The popular name for this masterpiece of civil architecture, *La Pedrera* («The Stone Quarry»), is due to the fact that during its construction the workers on the scaffolding would sculpt the stone façade according to Gaudí's instructions on site, looking like a quarry in the middle of the city. He personally supervised the work, just like he did with the meticulous laying of the ceramic pieces on the *Casa Batlló*. Even he himself, and not any of his collaborators, would create a model of a metallic balcony that, following the lines he had marked, would be carried out for the remaining balconies.

And this was how the façade of this house took its shape, like a stormy sea with a surface of metallic foam, a movement which was smoothly transferred to the inner courtyards and their rich polychromy or to the white roofs floating like ethereal clouds on the top of this unique and singular stone mountain. Or the ceilings of the different floors, which are like delicate lines of sand combed by the sea breeze and the sea currents. Once again, an abstract and tectonic formal conception governs Gaudí's design, never a conscious inclination towards figurative imitation. And this creation from abstraction, in Gaudí's case, can only be understood and deduced by somebody who is at the same time a critic-historian and an architect who actually designs and builds; therefore, an expert on internal creative processes and who also knows how to explain them. However, this is something that does not occur as frequently as it should regarding historiographers of modern architecture, which explains why our protagonist has been presented in an incomplete and even an untruthful manner. (Another thing is for the spectator to perceive the work from a figurative point of view, which does not interfere with the fact that his conception is from an abstract point of view or not.)

It is also important to bear in mind the use of terms such as *modernismo* (meaning *Art Nouveau* or *modern style*), *modernidad* (*Modernism*) and their respective adjectives - which lead to many a misunderstanding among Spanish-speakers-, and further confusion caused by the incorrect use of the adjective «sculptural» as a way of understanding architecture. It is even used incorrectly by some of the most famous critics, imbued with an extremely widespread rational-functionalist deformation, believing that «correct» architecture is only that which is material and objective, *sachlich*.

Artigas Gardens
1905, La Pobla de Lillet

Gaudí recreates the landscape through these gardens which span the River Llobregat and flank it on both banks; not as something created in a pre-existing natural landscape, but as the creation of a new landscape, where form and substance merge together in architecture, whilst during the same period, avant-garde painters and sculptors tried to do the same, learning from the Post-Impressionists.

53

Casa Milà
1906-1910/1911, Barcelona

This building marked the zenith of an architecture whose main characteristic is movement. Therefore, it was the privileged precursor of the whole futuristic avant-garde movement, which was born when this work was finished and whose aim was precisely that of incorporating movement as an abstract theme of art. It would also be a special model for what would soon after be known as German Expressionist architecture.

Casa Milà
1906-1910/1911, Barcelona

From the outside, the house has the appearance of caves dug into the rock, like genesiac nests, stone façades that conceal comfortable interiors; whereas the inside is covered with extremely delicate, soft vitelline skin-shaped forms. And although it proceeds from an abstract work, its enormous plasticity makes it transcend from the hermeticism characteristic of that abstraction to a popular level of communication.

Gaudí's work is one of the most affected by the use of the adjective «sculptural», as occurs in the case of *La Pedrera*. However, this or any other architectonic work cannot be called «sculptural» simply because it is complex, dynamic or figurative, just as a sculpture cannot be called «architectural» because it is simple, static or abstract. They are just different and must be described more accurately. Therefore, it is incorrect to state that the *Casa Milà* is «sculptural»; it would be better to say that, like the rest of his work, it is the fruit of Gaudí's ingenious plasticity. In other words, through his conciseness, his accuracy, and his power of expression, he manages to portray his mental images or ideas so well, to the extent that the public will understand his work as figurative and not hermetic and, therefore, as something close and agreeable.

The Sagrada Familia Provisional School
1908-1909, Barcelona

A small building of three connected classrooms each one corresponding with one of the three playgrounds outside, with their own drinking fountains, child-size benches and parabolic metallic and wire trelliswork which used to support heather, giving the place a certain exotic air. Gaudí also designed the furniture, using an ingenious combination of wood and iron.

The Sagrada Familia Provisional School, Barcelona, 1908-1909

A small, simple work, which is maybe why his ingeniousness is more enhanced. From the moment it was designed, it was destined to be an ephemeral building, since it was going to be later demolished as the ground was needed for building the ambulatory surrounding the whole church of the *Sagrada Familia*. According to the press of the time, the parish school was blessed and opened by the Bishop of Barcelona on 15th November, 1909, though by a photograph taken in 1908 we can see that at least the outside had been finished by this year. The fact that the bishop came to open such a tiny place shows the importance of this little work, in the zenith of his creative work, between the *Casa Batlló* and the *Casa Milà*, whilst his other key works were being built. This was the period in which the avant-garde artistic movements were emerging, a fact that places him in a precursory position.

Many great figures of modern architecture would be fascinated by this school building. For example, when Le Corbusier (1887-1965) travelled to Barcelona in 1928, he sketched it enthusiastically, being obvious inspiration for works of his such as the Philips Pavilion at the Brussels World Fair or Ronchamp Church. Those drawings by Le Corbusier would later be published in his *Complete Works* and in his book *Gaudí*. He was particularly interested in the system of brick vaulting, a characteristic of Catalonia and also something very present in Gaudí's work, as we can see here.

Due to the provisionality of this project, Gaudí designed a schematic, functional ground-plan, using the the cheapest building material on the market: typical Catalonian handmade thick ceramic brick, left undressed for greater economy. However, the result created such a stir that it became a milestone in the History of Architecture, due to its idea of space, its continuous unitary construction, not wedged in, and of a certain infinity, achieved only from an objective point of view.

The structure is the wall of enclosure itself and three beams placed vertically inside as columns which support another horizontal beam. They are all «I» –shaped metallic girders, which at the same time supported simple wooden

planks, like the ones used in the neighbouring work, on which the brick roof rests. These planks were placed, their inclination being varied accordingly, following an undulatory movement on the outside, which results in a geometrically undulating surface that follows the same curves of the pressures of its own loads. Likewise, the maximum stability of the carrying walls is achieved with the minimum of resources through its curvilinear ground-plan, with bricks, slanting as they go down. The bricks are arranged in a vertical manner, also the cheapest way of laying them, thus facilitating the wavy structure of the curves and increasing their strength. The result of intelligently achieving the maximum with the minimum is spectacular: delicate undulatory forms of great plasticity, which have been obtained by using functional and structural criteria, saving material, using only the strictly necessary to get the maximum physical and metaphysical result with the minimum cost and effort. This is what makes a genius.

The Sagrada Familia Provisional School
1908-1909, Barcelona

The windows would open by pivoting on a central horizontal axle, and all the openings were protected with a pediment made of undressed ceramic bricks. This work is in fact a reconstruction after it was destroyed by Anti-Christian groups that broke into the Sagrada Familia *Church. Neither have the original plans been preserved, being burnt together with all its files during those same terrorist acts.*

His Life's Work

The Sagrada Familia Church
1882/1883-1926/2032?, Barcelona
Scale model

A small scale model which shows us Gaudí's original design for this great work. Begun at the beginning of his professional career, as if it were just another work, it gradually absorbed him more and more, and he would be engaged on it throughout his whole life, his last years being entirely taken up by this project.

It is no mere coincidence that it was in 1883, the year in which he built his first houses (the *Casa Vicens* and *El Capricho*), that he received the commission that would last his whole life long, the work that would end up absorbing all his time and interest: the Church of the *Sagrada Familia*. This work would even transcend after his death, with the strong will of his disciples to complete it, and so fulfil their great master's desire for the church to be completed by his followers. This stage also has brought with it similar controversy to that suffered daily by the genius, since, whilst the common people are in favour (public surveys show that three out of every four wish the work to be continued), more than one intellectual has clearly stated otherwise. And in spite of the fact that this is the project which contains all his discoveries; the chronological study of the creative process of this building is the study of the evolution of all his architecture.

The Sagrada Familia Church, Barcelona, (1882-) 1883-1926 (-2032?)

In a photograph of the *Sagrada Familia* at the time of Antoni Gaudí's death, we can see exactly how much of the work had been completed to that date: during his life, he only saw the completion of one tower, that of *San Bernabé* (St. Barnabas). The other three would be finished between the date of his death and 1936, when the war (and then the hardships of the post-war period) paralysed the works, as well as the fact that revolutionaries destroyed sculptures, furniture and scale models, and burnt Gaudí's plans, drawings and files. They even opened his tomb in the crypt, but, fortunately, not his coffin. However, the nearby tomb of Josep María Bocabella was not so fortunate as his corpse did get desecrated; and the parish priest, Gil Parés, was murdered (1936).

Thanks to the retrieval of scattered pieces of the scale models and some drawings found elsewhere, it has been possible to gradually carry out an accurate reconstruction since Gaudí's methods were not arbitrary ones, but tended to follow the curved geometry, which allows for the reconstruction of the whole surface with just three points, as it responds to mathematical equations: something that helps to cut the stone accurately, thanks to an automatic machine whose computer is programmed with the corresponding equations of each piece.

The works have since continued and the other four towers and the naves have been completed; the only part still to be constructed is the main façade (on *Calle Mallorca*, which should be put underground) and the high domes. The central one, 173 m high (meaning that this would be the highest church in the whole of Christendom), is devoted to Jesus Christ, crowned with his symbol of the

The Sagrada Familia Church
1882/1883-1926/2032?, Barcelona
The Nativity façade

The explosion of life is represented here in a composition made up of grottos covered with
plants, animals, human beings and stars *which palpitate from the stone. Divided into three portals, each one referring to those scenes of the Life of Christ which are most identifiable with Faith, Hope and Charity, respectively.*

The Sagrada Familia Church
1882/1883-1926/2032?, Barcelona
Central scene of the Nativity façade

Representing the Birth of Jesus Christ and, therefore, the first moment in history in which the entire Holy Family (to whom this church is dedicated) would be seen together.

The Sagrada Familia Church
1882/1883-1926/2032?, Barcelona

Project started by Francisco de Paula del Villar (1828-1901), initially designed as a conventional Neo-Gothic church. However, several disagreements led to the architect's renunciation and its later commission to Gaudí. The latter would work on it during all his life, reaching the zenith of world religious architecture as the first modern cathedral, completely free from the traditional and Classical language of architecture.

cross, a four-armed one like those of Gaudí. Behind, the second highest, crowned with the star representing Virgin Mary.

Surrounding it, like in the *Tetramorphs* (traditional in Christian art) that accompanies the *Maiestas Domini*, four towers representing the Evangelists with each of their corresponding symbols. This does not fail to be an apocalyptic reference, since it is in the Book of the Apocalypse where those four winged-beings appear: the Human Being, Lion, Ox and Eagle, which were later assigned to each Evangelist, respectively, St. Matthew, St. Mark, St. Luke and St. John.

And then we have the eastern façade, the so-called «Nativity façade», looking to the east where the sun rises; and the more recent western façade, the «Death façade», built facing the west where the sun goes down (the two façades of the transept). The southern façade, the main one, yet to be built, the «Life» or «Glory» façade, is oriented south where the sun is in its zenith, in its «glory». All this corresponds to the cosmological symbols that constantly appear in his works; just like the twelve fruits (one representing each calendar month) that crown the façades of the naves, spring-summer ones on the eastern façade and autumn-winter ones on the western façade. The theological meaning of this corresponds to the twelve fruits of the Holy Ghost, which fructify in the souls when they come into contact with the Divine Grace, represented by twelve spotlights lighting them up from the towers.

On the three façades we have scenes depicting, respectively, Christ's Birth and Childhood, His Death and His Ascension to Heaven and His Return amidst clouds «in His Glory», as prophesied by the Apocalypse. These scenes give each façade its corresponding name, and are also a favourite artistic theme of Symbolist painters and sculptors: birth, life and death, or youth, adulthood and old age, here uniquely transferred to architecture. Three façades with four towers each, making a total of twelve, dedicated to the twelve Apostles. Once again, the image of the celestial Jerusalem of the Apocalypse, also depicted with twelve towers, one for each Apostle, crowned by the three symbols of the bishops, as they are the successors to the Apostles. Above, an open mitred shape; below, a polygonal-shaped ring with a hole for a finger; in between, a staff, whose curved shape goes from one side to the other in order to support the initial of each Apostle on the upper part of the tower; and, on the lower, we have statues of each of the Apostles flanked by their names.

The windows of the towers have downward projecting parts which were designed to act as resonators for the tubular bells that could be placed in the towers and which, as if they were huge pipes connected to an organ, could be heard throughout the whole city.

It is clear that Gaudí had designed an enormous total masterpiece, co-ordinating all the arts: music, as a huge organ with its towers and tiers designed for hundreds of singers; poetry-literature, with the theological-doctrinal meaning of each stone; theatre-dancing and scenic arts, through the theatre-show represented by the liturgy going on inside, since, after all, Catholic Mass is a representation of the Death of Jesus Christ; architecture, because of the building itself; sculpture, since it is everywhere, and painting, because he understood that it all had to be polychromed.

However, whilst he designed such a massive project, he was also capable of creating the minimum of details. For example, *Sanctus, Sanctus, Sanctus,* («Holy, Holy, Holy») a prayer devoted to the Holy Trinity that is placed winding its way around the towers, each in a different colour. The golden-yellow one is dedicated more to the divinity, the light, God the Father, the blood-red, to the martyrdom of God the Son; and the orange-coloured one to God the Holy Ghost who, according to the Catholic Church, comes from the Father and the Son, from the yellow and the red.

And, going even further, the Nativity façade contains scenes from Christ's childhood, with the natural exuberance of something new. In the middle of the scene of the Annunciation, with the Star of Bethlehem and the signs of the Zodiac as they appear in December: at the top left, Taurus, above it, Gemini, etc., dotted with the stars of a Christmas firmament.

The three portals of the façade are devoted to each one of the three most important Christian Virtues (Faith, Hope and Charity), and various scenes are portrayed accordingly. To the right, the Portal of Faith, with the Visitation, Jesus in the Temple, in the Workshop etc.; to the left, the Portal of Hope, with the Flight to Egypt, the Slaughter of the Holy Innocents, etc. The sculptures have been carried out by various authors and are of various qualities. Maybe the lowest-quality ones are those of the Adoration of the Shepherds, and the best, (amongst the old ones) those of the Visitation of the Virgin to her cousin St. Elizabeth, as well as the dramatism of the Slaughter of the Holy Innocents.

The Sagrada Familia Church
1882/1883-1926/2032?, Barcelona

In the middle and above the Nativity façade appears this enormous ceramic cypress tree, built after Gaudí's death. Crowned with a cross and held up by God's hand, it houses the white souls of the saints nesting in the form of white doves (the usual symbol of the soul) in the eternity symbolised by the evergreen cypress tree.

The Sagrada Familia Church
1882/1883-1926/2032?, Barcelona

The towers were designed as bell towers where tubular bells would resound, with downward-slanting pieces and openings which would act as huge sounding boards in directing the sound of the bells over the city. Winding their way around the towers are the words Sanctus, Sanctus, Sanctus *(«Holy, Holy, Holy»), which are addressed to the Holy Trinity, of which the Trinity of Earth, the Holy Family, is the symbol.*

However, since 1978 the quality of the sculptures on the façade of the *Sagrada Familia* has greatly improved due to the arrival of a great Japanese artist, Etsuro Sotoo (born 1953), who was following «the call of the stone», as he himself explains in a very Oriental way. This artist has become so influenced by Gaudí's way of thinking that he has converted to Catholicism, being baptised in this church. Not only do we owe him numerous figures of angels and children on the Nativity façade, but also the continuity of his dedication to the rest of the works, naves and transept. He is constantly engaged in the humble search for the correct interpretation and enrichment of the Gaudinian legacy.

Just like Gaudí, whilst bearing in mind the great magnitude of the façade, at the same time he ingeniously finds solutions, creating small details, such as the turtle and the tortoise that appear at its foot: the turtle indicates the «sea side» of the building, and the tortoise, the «mountain side». He thus reflects a popular way used by the inhabitants of Barcelona to locate themselves in the streets, using the terms «sea side» and «mountain side» for referring to the corresponding side of each street that is nearer the Mediterranean Sea or the Collserola mountains.

All this exuberance contrasts with the dramatic austerity of the «Death façade». In a drawing made of that façade by Gaudí we can also seen the theological distribution of the scenes of the Passion and Death of Jesus Christ, in relation not only to the three portals of Faith, Hope and Charity, but also to the Nativity façade. In this way, in the same place where the scene of Jesus' Birth is situated, that of His Death was also located, each one on its respective façade, thus closing a unitary cycle. Incomprehensibly, this has not been respected by those in charge of the works today, who have no better alternative and who are consequently destroying the subtle correspondence between stone and theology designed by Gaudí. The same can be said for the continuity of the works as a whole and of any work in general. The fact is that if they are not able to improve what has been previously established, then it would be preferable to carry on with the original plan and not make it worse with something new.

The sculptures here are by Josep María Subirachs (born 1927), who decided to change the original situation with regard to the unpublished theological study of Gaudí concerning their simple chronological distribution (as he himself explains), following a great «S» for Subirachs. Also, in the work carried out by An-

The Sagrada Familia Church
1882/1883-1926/2032?, Barcelona
The Death façade

In contrast with the Nativity façade with its explosion of life in its many forms, this one is reduced to the rigor mortis *of simple, unadorned lines. Recently the sculptures here have been the centre of controversy due to the unnaturalness and lack of piety of the figures and the changes incorporated by the sculptor Josep Maria Subirachs. For example, the scene of Christ's Death at the top is not in the place originally projected by Gaudí.*

toni Tàpies (born 1923), the «T» prevails. (The latter is as important to Catalonian painting as the former is to Catalonian architecture).

The sculptures on this façade reflect all the pessimism of suffering and death, the finest probably being the first one completed, before the controversy arose due to their discrepancy with the rest of Gaudí's ensemble and their unsuitableness for fulfilling their religious function of leading to Christian piety. The first sculpture is that of the Scourging of Jesus, where the sculptor came across a palm fossil when carving it, a plant that symbolises martyrdom, and which he considered to be a providential finding. However, it does seem to be somewhat impertinent the fact that he consecrated the shape of the chimney pots on the *Casa Milà* representing the helmets of the Roman soldiers who took part in the Crucifixion of Jesus Christ, however abstract they may be, without any figurative intention. And now, the Death façade looks like a parade of the *Casa Milà* chimney pots. It would be more correct (more Gaudinian) to say that they are «mushrooms» and not helmets, as a conclusive reply to the spreading of such imaginative deviations, after carrying out a serious interpretative-formal study of the chimneys on Gaudí's houses.

On the other hand, all the façades are surrounded by a corridor-cloister, also designed as a place to say the Rosary, its 50 beads being represented three times on the façade. (This makes us remember how the roads at Güell Park (flanked by 150 huge seat-balls) are turned into a great big Rosary). The cloister surrounds the whole building, through the spaces forming the three façades, creating a parallel with the 15 Mysteries of the Rosary, each one made up of 10 *Ave Marias* (small rosary beads) (with the result that a Rosary has 50 beads which are counted three times). The Nativity façade contains scenes of the five Mysteries of Joy; the Death façade shows the five Mysteries of Sorrow, and that of the Glory, suggests the so-called Mysteries of Glory of the Rosary.

The Sagrada Familia Church
1882/1883-1926/2032?, Barcelona
Windows

*This view corresponds with the side windows
of the most recently built naves, still lacking*

*their respective stained glass. They are
composed of intersections of hyperboloids, as
the surfaces which best convey light, and
paraboloids. The architects who have taken
over the construction work have been helped
by high-tech computer-designed plans.*

The Sagrada Familia Church
1882/1883-1926/2032?, Barcelona
Vaults and pillars in the central naves

*Pillars branch upwards and slant,
following the catenary lines, i.e. seeking the
exact direction of the natural loads of the
ceiling. The surfaces that best transport
them are those which join them without
solution of continuity, by means of curved
geometry, paraboloids and hyperboloids.*

On this long journey, a metaphor of our own life, with its joys and sorrows, different doors are dedicated to various Marian invocations. The most joyful ones are on the Nativity façade, the Virgin of the Rosary and the Virgin of Montserrat (the patroness of Barcelona). And on the Death façade, those of Our Lady of Sorrow and Our Lady of Mercy (patroness of the diocese of Barcelona), the latter being connected with the hard task of freeing slaves. Meanwhile, the cloister is presided over by the chapel dedicated to the Assumption of the Virgin Mary, the last dogma laid down by the Catholic Church. All this is no more than the reflection of Gaudí's own devotion to saying the Rosary, since the Catholic Church recommends it as the most excellent of prayers dedicated to the Virgin Mary, and that is why such great protagonism is given to it by the author of this church.

It is also interesting to point out its Latin cross ground-plan, and that the five naves each have a main entrance, each one respectively representing five of the Seven Sacraments. Two chapels at the entrance of the church are dedicated to the other two sacraments, those of purification, so that worshippers may, before entering the church, first go into the chapel that best satisfies their spiritual needs, whether that of Baptism (symbolised by water and a large fountain in front) or that of Confession (symbolised by fire and a torch).

And inside these five naves, the slanting pillars and their branching out, made of reinforced concrete covered in granite, basalt or porphyry, according to the structural resistance required. They bear the weight of the ceiling, rising up to the zenithal light coming through hyperboloid-shaped openings, which are those which best let the light through. The finishing touch is achieved by the installation of alabaster lamps, which, together with the soft rays of moonlight, illuminate these spaces at night-time. The final result inside the church creates the atmosphere of a peaceful forest, with light faintly filtering through its leaves and branches. And all this comes from constructive logic in harmony with functions, forms and discourse, which only Gaudí has been able to synthesise.

Arts and Crafts

This could be a motto, written in letters of gold or carved in marble, of the design and architecture of Antoni Gaudí, key words which prevail in all his works. This motto is in line with the awakening of «modernity», first in Great Britain, and the movement for the reformation of applied arts that would end up being known by this term, the purpose of which being to increase the quality of crafts by conferring them artistic sensibility. With the result that Gaudí was personally in contact with each artisan who collaborated with him.

«Arts and Crafts» is also the term with which the *Bauhaus* was formed in Germany in 1919, until it was replaced by «Arts and Techniques» in 1923. The *Bauhaus*, which was the paradigmatic school of modernity, pioneer in the teaching of avant-garde principles of art, architecture and design. And so we have Gaudí, situated chronologically and conceptually between the decline of the nineteenth-century Arts and Crafts movement and the arrival of the modern *Bauhaus*.

Stonework

It is true to say that Gaudí did not count on the regular and inestimable collaboration of the best stone sculptors of the day, especially if we compare his situation with that of Lluís Domènech, who did, however, have the greatest figures of Catalonian Modernism working with him: Eusebi Arnau (1864-1933), Miquel Blay (1866-1936), Pau Gargallo (1881-1934)…

This confirms to what extent Gaudí's work was more personal, whilst that of Lluís Domènech, and even that of Josep Puig, was more dependent on a team of brilliant artists who were all devoted to applied arts. Apart from specific collaborations on the part of Josep Llimona (1864-1934), one of the contemporary sculptors most present in his works, Carles Mani (1866-1911), Llorenç and Joan Matamala (respectively, 1856-1927 and 1893-1977) are the most outstanding. (After Gaudí's death, others still carry on the sculpturing work of the *Sagrada Familia* Church). These three artists are of quite a different level to that of the previously-mentioned ones, if we compare the work of each one. However, under the direction of Gaudí their skill grew and he managed to get

The Sagrada Familia Church
1882/1883-1926/2032?, Stonework from the Slaughter of the Holy Innocents, Barcelona

Indeed one of the most dramatic scenes of the whole work, stressed by the fact that it is found on the Portal of Hope of the pleasant Nativity façade. Together with the figures, there are natural forms of plants and animals typical of Palestine and Christmas sculpted as if they were living walls.

Casa Milà
1906-1910/1911, Stonework, Barcelona

A typical detail in Gaudí's works which were closely monitored by him. Here, as on other columns, abstract forms, small flowers, anagrams and words with various interpretations will be sculpted. For example, there is nothing more appropriate for a dining room than delicately sculpted pieces of fruit.

the best out of them. This is also applicable to the rest of his collaborators, to the extent that the stonework that Gaudí designed for his works goes much further, insofar as proposals, creation and innovation are concerned, than the rest of his contemporary architects, being ahead of them on the road to abstraction. Still absorbed as they were in understanding stonework from a merely decorative, floral and even Classicising point of view, depending on the case. Many of them would end up going back to Noucentist Classicism. And that is precisely the main difference: Gaudí *works with* the stone and the rest simply *work* the stone.

This more essentialising and tectonic way of carrying out architecture is particularly noticeable on the carved stone façades of the *Casa Batlló* and *Casa Milà*. A whole generation has been skipped, and with the materic perversion of *Casa Batlló* and the futuristic dynamism of the *Casa Milà*, he advances towards an understanding that is more characteristic of artistic avant-garde movements than of his days. The soft, fleshy forms of the *Casa Batlló* supported by thin sticks fascinated Dalí, who made paintings and sculptures of a similar kind, enthusiastic about that architecture which he considered to be protosurrealist. Dalí himself remarked how the architecture of the future would be like that of Gaudí, «soft»

and «hairy». The soft waves on the *Casa Milà*, some of them superimposed on the metallic waves, would also be a source of inspiration for Expressionist architects.

On the other hand, in the *Sagrada Familia* Church, together with the necessary sculptures on religious themes, natural plant and animal motifs abound, sprouting from the sculpted stone, forming living walls, antecedents in stone to genetic architecture. And, the same as in the conception of the *Sagrada Familia*, the simultaneous approach of the great architectonic concept and the slightest detail, visible, for example, on the pillars inside the *Casa Milà*, in the way of ab-

Casa Batlló
1904-1906, Stonework, Barcelona

Unique stonework in the form of extremely slender pillars. Gaudí made dreams the subject of his architecture, and, here, the result looks like a cave mouth, a reminiscent of the primitive home.

In his woodwork, Gaudí displays the same delicacy seen in his stonework, the same vitality shown in his ceramics and the same skill proved in his ironwork. Fortunately, a great part of the furniture and fittings designed by Gaudí for his Calvet, Batlló and Milà houses are faithfully commercialised from Barcelona.

stract forms, delicate flowers, religious anagrams and whole words with different interpretative versions.

Woodwork

It is in the furniture designed by Gaudí for his buildings, as well as in the carpentrywork, frames and doors of his *Casa Calvet*, *Casa Batlló* and *Casa Milà*, where one can best appreciate his craftsmanship in wood. And, once again, it is Gaudí himself, and not collaborating artists, who personally designs these items down to the minimum detail and supervises their production. The final result will not attract our attention due to the delicate and laborious inlaid work of various types of wood and precious materials, which was customary on the part of artists working for other important architects. Gaspar Homar (1870-1953) would be the most exquisite example of this, who frequently collaborated with Lluís Domènech.

In this sense, Gaudí's work is more simple and modern. Its spectacularity above all resides in the constructive ingeniousness of his creation, its typological renovation and his curious way of incorporating the metal fittings. And all this can be seen right from the start, in the *Casa Vicens*. And then we have the plasticity of the final result, as if the items had been designed by nature itself. Naturally, there is an enormous difference between his first furniture and the last.

Casa Batlló
1904-1906, Woodwork, Barcelona
Bench

As if cast from the human body, its ergonomic design at the service of comfort and its modern functionality are well ahead of a period still dominated by Classical aesthetics. The plastic forms of the bench are pleasant and interesting: they are therefore an alternative to Classicism and the coldness of the Rationalism-Functionalism inspired by the world of machines.

At the beginning, many of his works were of a complex and heavy aspect, rather showy and weird-looking, and also of a vague mediaeval style which fascinated him. Over the years, we can observe how his style becomes more and more refined, concentrating more on a clean and intelligent tectonicity, on a unitary organicity, and on a dynamic and abstract plasticity. The consequence is a final product with a lighter and a more gracious appearance; and always with a perfect ergonomical-functional design, even before such a term had been invented. That is why his chairs are indeed extremely comfortable, being perfectly adapted to the human body, as if the latter had been used as a mould. It is true to such an extent that, bearing in mind the differences between the male and the female anatomies, especially taking into account the pompous dresses of those days, he had the intention of designing a different chair for each sex, something that was considered ridiculous at the time, in spite of the anthropomorphic logic of the matter. Things have not changed much since then: to this day, nobody has yet commercialised chairs for each sex.

Like in its architecture, the furniture of the *Casa Calvet* acts as a hinge for the turn of the century, featuring, on the one hand, forms of his early stages, but also introducing new ones which would gradually become predominant in all Gaudí's work. Therefore, in the same house we can see wooden benches of both kinds, some sturdier and more rectilinear, and others whose freshness, svelteness and brightness surprise us. The latter is the style that triumphs in his following works, for example in the *Casa Batlló* and *Casa Milà*, and which would give Gaudí international fame.

This uniqueness, together with the organicity of the material and the product, and the way he evokes abstract forms of nature, will lead other architects such as Carlo Mollino (1905-1978) and Óscar Tusquets (born 1941) to taking inspiration from him and designing their *Gaudí* and *Gaulino* chairs, respectively.

Ceramics

With regard to this material, leaving aside his frequent use of ceramic brick, Gaudí introduced a key system which would end up be extremely successful.

El Capricho
1883-1885, Ceramics, Comillas
Sunflowers

The motif chosen here by Gaudí, the sunflower, corresponds with a plant of great symbolism: it is a flower which follows the direction of the sun and even looks like it, with its big round centre and its golden-rayed petals. Once again, Gaudí is ahead of his time, anticipating the use of the sunflower by Symbolists, going from Van Gogh to the German and Austrian Secessionists.

First of all, because many artists would apply it, both those of his time (Lluís Domènech, Josep Maria Jujol, Josep Puig ...) and of ours (Santiago Calatrava, Alberto Estévez, Eduard Samsó ...). And, going even further, we could say that this system is also the one which graphically identifies the figure of Gaudí and even the entire Catalonian Modernist movement.

This is why, taking advantage of its evocative power which has become so popular, it has been used on numerous occasions, events, in all kinds of establishments, logotypes, items and souvenirs. We are talking about *trencadís*, (meaning «breakable/fragile» in the Catalan language, from *trencar*, «break»), used to talk about the mosaics composed of broken ceramic tiles. This is something which he used from the very beginning, for example in the Güell Stables, where the

Güell Park
1900-1914, Ceramics, Barcelona
Dragon

The nowaday toothless and inoffensive dragon at the entrance underwent drastic tooth surgery when what was going to be a private housing estate became a public park, the once dangerously-looking jaws being suddenly put within the reach of children. However, Gaudí's colourful and ingenuous talent has made him the precursor of the most naïve *part of so many artists, from Joan Miró to Niki de Saint-Phalle.*

trencadís is used on the hyperboloids of the roofs or subtly between the different bricks, thus colouring their joints with tiles instead of leaving the cement visible. Maybe this is the origin of the *trencadís*, the idea of colouring the joints of cement (which is also of two different colours), because even the small square pieces of Roman mosaics which he incorporates into his works would have to have been broken up to fit into such a small space. Whichever the origin, the system adapts perfectly to the undulating surfaces of his architecture, with the great advantage that, being irregular polygonal forms, the normal dilations of the pieces due to day-to-day changes in temperature do not add up in a linear way, but counteract mutually, solving one of the critical problems of applying regular ceramic elements outside.

Although the *trencadís* and the configurations achieved with it are present in all his work, resolving practically any covering and detail with that system, it is not the only type of ceramic element designed by Gaudí, for example the daisies on the *Casa Vicens*, the sunflowers on *El Capricho*, the sunflowers on the *Casa Batlló* and, naturally, on the *Sagrada Familia* Church, in the form of doves and cypress leaves. Of course, they will be the exception, especially when we compare Gaudí with other authors of his time who usually commissioned the production of their tiles to others, not making them on site which is the case of the *trencadís*. Moreover, this method can save a lot of money, since the material used may cost nothing, even coming from waste or recycled (before this term was invented) objects, and the labour does not necessarily have to be specialised.

The most powerful reason for the use of tiles is that it allows to introduce chromatism into his works, something that was vital for Gaudí. The durability of its colour is practically eternal, in comparison with the polychromy of stone, wood and iron.

Ironwork

It has already been observed how his ironwork, from the very beginning in buildings such as *El Capricho*, is the protagonist. Gaudí, by far, knew how to make the best and most out of this material, from his early days. This is even more evident if we compare this fact with the works of his greatest contemporary artists, for example Lluís Domènech, Josep Puig and even Josep Maria Jujol. In spite of the high quality of the first two artists' works in stone, their first works in iron (the most modern material) are wrought in a rougher manner and their design is much more limited. This fact becomes all the more evident when we compare these works with the originality, freshness and skill with which Gaudí achieves his design, spatiality and construction.

This is greatly due to the fact that the latter was the son of a coppersmith, consequently spending much of his childhood in his father's workshop, as he himself admitted, allowing him to acquire a special knowledge of working with metal. He understood that it was there that his enormous ability to imagine the three dimensions was developed, when contemplating the curved surfaces acquired by the cauldrons (in this case, made of copper) during their production process. Something similar occurred with Adolf Loos (1870-1933), who spent his childhood in his father's stonemason's workshop, which, in turn, would give this artist a special sensibility for choosing and combining different types of marbles and understanding their textures, (as we can clearly observe in his works).

The first great surprise which Gaudí gave us in this respect was when he created the spectacular iron dragon of the gate to the Güell Stables. To begin with, here we have an example of all the ways in which iron can be wrought: plate, bar, with profiles, in the form of a chain and a spiral, cast, welded, hammered

The Güell Stables
1884-1887, Ironwork, Barcelona
Dragon

With the dragon as the supreme symbol of evil, an element present in the whole of Gaudí's

work, he represents all the horror and dreadfulness of the dark side of man; always exposed in an architectural key, which would later be particularly developed by the most Nihilist artists of Expressionism, especially by artists such as Alfred Kubin.

Güell Palace
1885-1888/1890, Ironwork
Barcelona

By way of a coat of arms, something usual on palace entrances, he places the four stripes of Catalonia-Aragón achieved by ingeniously winding them round a cylinder; above this, a helmet with a winged dragon on the top, which corresponds, according to Juan Bassegoda, with the contraction of d'Aragó («of Aragón»).

or screwed. And all this in accordance with a good, fluid and natural design, with natural forms, where each part is in the right position, each one being represented in perfect harmony with the rest. It is an unforgettable lesson, which shows us his skill in ironwork from the very start of his career. This early mastership was constantly improved, until it reached its maximum expression on the grilles, railings and balconies of *Casa Milà*. He himself would prepare a natural-scale sample of these balconies and give it to the forgers as a model. Of course, whenever he got the chance, he would also use iron as a structural material, as we can see in Count Güell's Palace, the *Casa Botines, Casa Calvet* or *Casa Milà*.

We cannot forget to highlight the exquisite and complex ironwork at Count Güell's Palace, *Casa Calvet* or *Casa Batlló* or the gates and bars of the *Teresian Schools, Casa Botines*, Count Güell's Stables or *Bellesguard*. Each and every one of the same quality, harmony and mastership that have already been mentioned. Many are the studies published which corroborate his singular career, in a constant and perfectly comprehensible evolution, without any solution of continuity.

Sources of Inspiration

History of Art is the history of human fascinations, those which have dazzled its main protagonists and which have illuminated the way to find the sources that allow them to develop their creative act. And writing about those attractions is a fascinating task.

Also, in the case of Gaudí, his personal fascinations are easily deduced from his work, behind which his sources of inspiration palpitate. «Man moves in a world of two dimensions, and angels in a three-dimensional one. Sometimes, after many sacrifices, sharp and continuous pain, the architect manages to get a momentary glimpse of the angelic tridimensionality. The architecture that is born from this inspiration produces results that satisfy generations.» These are Gaudí's words, taken from Joan Bergós' book *Gaudí, el hombre y la obra.*

Therefore, a way of understanding him would be to try to investigate those superhuman «flashes» that he sensed, his likely sources of inspiration. Naturally, in such a restless person there are many different and maybe unconscious ones. However, they always lead to an effective movement of architectural creation, and that is why they can be inferred.

Some are so precise that they are immediately turned into constructive detail, such as the architectonic treatment that he gives to the corners of his buildings, transforming them ingeniously into spaces. Or the layout of the entrance to his buildings, in the form of a protruding, almost free-standing pavilion designed as a place to welcome or say goodbye to its users, just like in the *Casa Vicens, El Capricho* and in the Episcopal Palace.

Other fascinations are more ethereal ones which may be observed, for example, in the religious-symbolic meaning of his architecture. Or in the globalising will that he will fuse, each time better, the most objective and the most subjective strata in an architectural unit.

So, here we have an insight into some Gaudinian invariants. To begin with, which would be the first non-physiological sensation (i.e. neither hunger, thirst, cold, etc.) of the human being? The feeling of space: in the mother's womb, one is aware of being in a peaceful, cosy space, which is also self-sufficient, protected and secure, controlling one's limits and dimensions, and feeling the vitelline membrane. It is a space, as Dalí says when referring to his intra-uterine memories, which feels like Paradise, but which also has the colours of Hell: pinks, reds, yellows and oranges, the natural colours of the mother's skin and blood, which is translucent. (The epithelial folds on the ceilings of *Casa Milà* turn out to be very revealing in this respect.) The space of paradisiac sensations which one tries to retrieve after being born between the hollows of the body, in one's mother's arms, under the blankets of the cradle; or by building a den, something that he certainly must have done during his childhood.

Casa Milà
1906-1910/1911, Ironwork, Barcelona
Balconies

*The abstract way in which he would work
with iron, which can be observed throughout*
*the whole city of Barcelona, with balconies as
its maximum exponent, would also have its
direct influence on the most important local
avant-garde sculptors, such as Pau Gargallo
and Julio González and, therefore, on all
later artists.*

The Güell Colony Church
1898/1908-1917, Barcelona
Windows

Brightly-coloured stained-glass windows, some of which remind us of butterflies with open wings, due to their layout and their symmetrical way of opening. His geometric designs, especially in their naïve strokes and colours, are in line with those of artists such as Henri Matisse and Marc Chagall.

Casa Milà
1906-1919/1911, Barcelona

At the sight of this «mountain-house», it would be useless to say that it was designed in an abstract way, as the creation of a new reality, not copied from anything else, and along the same conceptual lines of work as those defined by Apollinaire for Cubism. One immediately thinks of possible inspiration coming from the hills of Montserrat or the Sierra de Fra Guerau, which he knew well, or even Cappadocia, which he never visited.

The Teresian School
1888-1889, Barcelona

The catenary-parabolic arch is the protagonist of an also objective and material architecture, which is concerned about its constructive logic and rationality, and finds its effectiveness in the pragmatism of Catalonian tradition and civil engineering which use it. The immediate consequence is to move away from the historical styles of the past as none of them featured this kind of arch. Therefore, if the so-longed-for modern style had to be characterised by an arch, then it would be this one.

But the innate sensation of lost paradise and happiness will be recorded forever in the deepest part of the soul, whilst one strives to recuperate it during our earthly existence. A possible reflection of this is the frequent appearance in his projects of hollows, small caverns, tiny, cosy, pleasant spaces, made to measure the human body. From the *Casa Vicens* to the Church of the *Sagrada Familia*, which is completely made up of grottos. This primitive conduct can end up being almost a compulsive instinct, equally detectable in other authors. The most evident example of this tendency in other contemporary architects would be Hans Hollein (born 1934).

Secondly, when one thinks of leaving those comfortable inner spaces, the need arises to be protected from the unknown and threatening outside. This makes the skin enclosing these inhabitable caves sense that they need to be protected from the outside, by strongly-built defences, which explains how his works can be understood through the typology of fortresses, together with his inspiration by the Middle Ages. This is something that has been corroborated work after work, however ludicrous it may seem: solid, mostly made of stone, with moats, towers and well-defined crenellations, spiky gates and doors, where, once again, from the *Casa Vicens* to the church of the *Sagrada Familia*, including the *Casa Milà*, they even have parapets, something that is more characteristic of fortresses than houses.

That limit between the outside and the inside and the need for such «defences» explains the figure of the dragon —the outside being full of them. Dragons appear frequently in Gaudí's works: from the design of his architect's desk itself, which he places as a perpetual reminder around it in an attacking pose, although they also form «G» for Gaudí. It is also interesting, in order to illustrate this idea of dragons as perturbing elements prowling around outside, to point out that the most extreme sculptures on the Nativity façade of the *Sagrada Familia* Church are, to the right and to the left, two dragon-like reptiles, showing that evil is outside the «sacred space» of that façade. The same goes for the dragon-like snakes on the entrance to the Güell Palace.

Of course, there are always dragons and reptiles «behind the scenes», as the most representative and most ancient symbols of evil, although parallel explanations can be found in Classic mythology or related with Catalonia and its mediaeval traditions. They also have a nationalist meaning, in line with the strong revival of the Catalonian nationalist sentiment at that time, which could not be ignored by architects or politicians. This explains why the figure of St. George appears so frequently in works, even if it was only because he is the patron saint of Catalonia, identified with the slaying of the dragon. However, the full version is that, as the patron of Catalonia, St. George slays the dragon of centralism in order to free the country, represented by the maiden that has been captured by the dragon. Along these lines, and related with Gaudí's communicative effectiveness, Juan Bassegoda tells us about a French politician who once came to give a conference invited by the Athenaeum of Barcelona; of how, when passing in front of the *Casa Milà*, he was immediately petrified by the deadly breath of the beast, and how he fled back to his country without attending the conference, saying what a terrible place Catalonia was, a land whose people constructed dwellings for dragons.

However, throughout the whole 20th century and until now, it has been proved that this world of «dragons and dungeons» has always been present in regional folklore, having been developed by the publishing and film industry due to its great demand. It is no passing fashion. Although it may appear to be contradictory with modernity, it is something that has always been there and at least the youngest generations are still interested in this secular genre of «magic and swords». In this way, Gaudí is the modern architect (and almost the only one) who has best recreated those human dreams architecturally.

Another factor that helps us to understand his works is detecting, after reviewing his projects, how, in his early stages, he used historical styles as sources of inspiration, although academicists would throw their hands to their heads when they saw what he was doing. He did not use these elements in a very orthodox way, reconstructing them to create his personal style of architecture. Besides, he never used what historicists consider to be something which defines a style: its arches. The only exception is the ogive, which he did use at the beginning of his career with a Gothic style, keeping in line with the teachings of Eugène-Emmanuel Viollet-Le-Duc regarding his understanding of structural appropriateness.

He would design his own arch, the catenary one, his own constructive system, which was neither traditional nor identifiable with any other style. Only civil engineers starting from Physical Science and Catalonian masons from popular experience have been able to approach the catenary arch, since it is the one which is most consistent with the natural functioning of structures. And it would

Güell Colony Church
1898/1908-1917, Barcelona
Scale model

This corresponds to the structural study for this church, which would also be useful to Gaudí later on for making quicker progress in his project of the Sagrada Familia. *All one needs to do is to turn this photograph upside down and one will immediately see, as if by magic, how the catenary arches, the vaults, the domes and the towers of this project were to be carried out following strict scientific logic and constructive economy.*

be Gaudí, from his artistic rationality, who would be the first to introduce it into learned architecture.

If we compare his works with those of his contemporaries, the compositive difference is so great that it is evident that he only drew inspiration from styles, but did not merely imitate them as the eclecticists did. And when he eventually got all he could out of these sources, at the same time as new ones arose, he achieved his masterpieces, those works that have made him famous, and which anticipated later artistic movements. This is probably due to the fact that his definitive source of inspiration was nature, whether the mineral kingdom (e.g. the cliff-like walls of the *Casa Milà*), the vegetable kingdom (e.g. the roofs evoking lichens and mushrooms in Güell Park) or the animal kingdom (e.g. the butterfly-shaped windows of the Güell Colony Church). This inspiration can also be observed in the structures of his works, since they are in keeping with the same criteria of tectonic functionality as those of nature. By following them, he succeeded in applying maximum structural efficiency to traditional compression architecture, at the same time as he initiated modern traction architecture.

For instance, he introduced the unbeatable catenary-parabolic arch as an alternative to the deficient static performance of historic-style arches, which presented the same problems from roofs and vaults to walls and pillars. His arch, turned into a surface by successive repetition (the Gaudinian diaphragmed space is simply this), running through space, but along a second curvature opposed to its own and of similar geometry, solved the problem. These catenary arches and

their nearness to the parabola, their corresponding undulating vaults and slanting pillars following the same natural direction of the load of the upper weights, obtain the ideal structural work in a building, with a minimum amount of material. Gaudí succeeded in «putting the finishing touch» to the millenary History of Architecture and compression construction.

Besides, these curved forms abound in nature, in whose evolution the most appropriate structural geometries have been selected so that plants and bones may be as strong as possible by using the minimum. Cubes do not exist in nature, but ellipsoids, hyperboloids and paraboloids, in stalks, trunks and branches and in every apparatus of all living beings. Gaudí would say: «My ideas are of unquestionable logic, and I simply cannot understand how they have not been applied before, and why it falls to me to be the first to lead the way. It is the only thing which makes me sometimes hesitate.»

But later architects did acknowledge such merits, for instance, Le Corbusier, who said: «What a fantastic mastery of structures: this man is certainly the best architect of his generation!»

Casa Milà
1906-1910/1911, Barcelona
Interior

Here we have the upper floor of La Pedrera *(«the quarry»), whose diaphragmed space with its display of catenary arches is frequent in Gaudí's works. It is now that we can understand how spaces like the Güell Stables or the Teresian School are antecedents of this, but in a simpler and more linear style, still lacking the organicist unitary perfection achieved during these years.*

The Sagrada Familia Provisional School
1908-1909, Barcelona

This small building once again corroborates the fact that Gaudí's work is the precursor of all the curved geometry forms that Naum Gabo and Antoine Pevsner would use in their creation of Abstract sculpture, or that would, many years later, come into fashion with the work of Pier Luigi Nervi and Félix Candela, to name just a couple of examples of architecture.

Casa Milà
1906-1910/1911, Barcelona
Floor tiles

Designed by Gaudí and produced by Casa Escofet *as a hydraulic mosaic, it had been initially projected for the* Casa Batlló, *but in fact was laid in the* Casa Milà, *thus confirming the influence of the natural Mediterranean landscape in both projects. The tiles are of a soft green sea colour, have delicate naturalist sea forms and an ingenious hexagonal composition.*

Of course, in order to have such efficient inspiration one must have a true love of and be sincerely fascinated by nature. Gaudí always worked in harmony with nature, respecting the immediate surroundings and the environment, to the extent that we could call him the first environmentalist architect, at a time when this term did not even exist. This is the utmost synthesis of Gaudí's architecture, somebody who first goes through all the historical styles, giving them the finishing touch (the same as when one is about to die, one briefly recalls all one's life), introducing all architectural styles into his works over a very short period (Greco-Roman, Romanesque, Gothic, Renaissance, Baroque, Near and Far East-

Casa Calvet
1898-1899, Woodwork
Barcelona
Bench and chair

It is above all in the furniture and the fittings of this house, and in details like the upper balconies, in other words, all which is designed at the end, where the radical change that Gaudí's work experienced at the turn of the century can best be seen. One goes from the sources of inspiration coming from history to those of nature and its geometry, and so he finally discovers the great modern alternative.

ern ...). He developed these styles to perfection, art-wise and technique-wise, with their definitive structural and formal improvement, discovering that it corresponds with the precise functioning of the natural world.

And, on corroborating such an identification artifice-nature, he anticipated the new modern tradition, his works displaying characteristics of Expressionism, Futurism, Abstractionism, Surrealism, Organicism, using *collage, assemblage* and *dripping* as techniques typical of avant-garde tendencies, of Brutalism, Informalism and Povera art, and anticipating Postmodern irony in the use of history. They are all sketches, outlines, first attempts of the same modern language which takes over from five millenniums of the development of what is known as the Classical language of architecture.

Chromatic Architecture

All of Gaudí's projects were conceived bearing very much in mind their colours. «There's no fooling the people; when one sees a person with a very pale complexion, one says that he looks as pale as death, and when one sees a dead body with rosy cheeks one says that it looks as if it were alive», quotes Joan Bergós in *Gaudí, el hombre y la obra.*

Colour is life, he would say, and life is colour, therefore: what is alive has colour as life implies colour. With an idea of colour that goes much further than

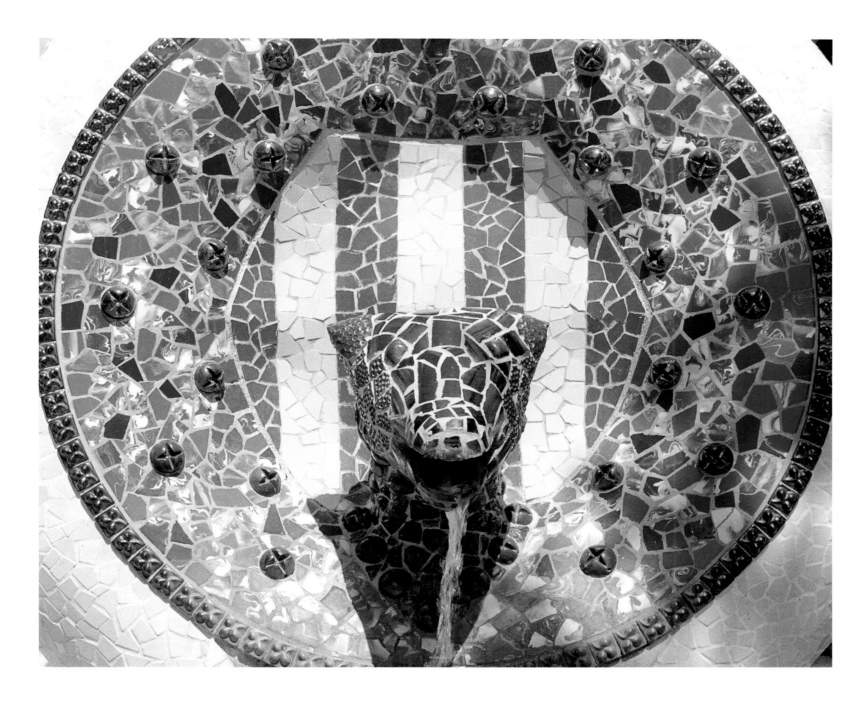

the mere optical phenomenon. Giving colour to life also has that figurative meaning which architecture is able to reflect and which Gaudí's architecture does reflect. For him, it was, once again a question of logic … . If nature, and everything surrounding us, is so brightly coloured, then what about architecture? And even more so if it is lively architecture, as full of vital energy and spirit as his. In this more metaphysical sense his architecture would be chromatic.

Colour is everywhere, even in the unity achieved and its spatial movement; life flows fully and chromatically through the stone, wooden, ceramic and iron tectonicity, and on a level that goes far beyond a merely physical and material one, fruit of his inner joy which shows through the coloured echoes of Gaudinian symbols.

Politicians, clergymen, citizens of all classes, creeds and races should pay the maximum tribute to Gaudí; and those awards, titles and prizes should gladden us all, whatever our origin and our beliefs, for what he has done in the common interest mankind with his life and works.

Güell Park
1900-1914, Ceramics
Barcelona

Another lively and colourful piece, so frequent in his work, especially achieved with his usual technique of trencadís *of ceramic fragments which ensure an almost eternal colour, without the need to be painted and repainted. However, this chromatic will transcends beyond simple objective and material optical effects, creating a genuine chromatic architecture also from a subjective and a spiritual point of view.*

BIBLIOGRAPHY

BASSEGODA, Juan: *Antonio Gaudí. Vida y Arquitectura.* Barcelona, 1977.

BASSEGODA, Juan: *Gaudí. Arquitectura del futuro.* Barcelona, 1984.

BASSEGODA, Juan: *El Gran Gaudí.* Sabadell, 1989.

BASSEGODA, Juan: *Aproximación a Gaudí.* Aranjuez, 1994.

BASSEGODA, Juan, y COLLINS, George R.: *The Designs and Drawings of Antonio Gaudí.* Princeton, 1983.

BENEVOLO, Leonardo: *Historia de la arquitectura moderna.* Barcelona, 1974.

BERGÓS, Joan: *Gaudí, el hombre y la obra.* Barcelona, 1974.

CASTÁN, Patricia: *Los barceloneses se rinden a Gaudí,* in *El Periódico.* Barcelona, 26 August, 1997.

CATALOGUE *Gaudí* (1852-1926). Exhibition of the Fundació Caixa de Pensions, Barcelona, 1984.

COLLINS, George R.: *Antonio Gaudí.* New York, 1960.

ESTÉVEZ, Alberto Tomás: *Destrucción versus construcción,* in *La Mañana.* Lleida, 10 April, 1994.

ESTÉVEZ, Alberto Tomás: *De Gaudí a Calatrava,* in *D'Art,* no 22. Barcelona, 1996.

ESTÉVEZ, Alberto Tomás: *El equipo de la Sagrada Familia,* in *AB: Arquitectes de Barcelona,* No 61. Barcelona, 1998.

ESTÉVEZ, Alberto Tomás: *Tres de cada quatre barcelonins pensen que les obres del Temple s'han de continuar,* in *Temple,* No 132. Barcelona, 1998.

FLORES, Carlos: *Gaudí, Jujol y el Modernismo catalán.* Madrid, 1982.

GÜELL, Xavier: *Antoni Gaudí.* Barcelona, 1986.

LE CORBUSIER : *Gaudí.* Barcelona, 1967.

MARTINELL, César: *Gaudí: su vida, su teoría, su obra.* Barcelona, 1967.

MUÑOZ, María Teresa: *La otra arquitectura orgánica.* Madrid, 1995.

PANE, Roberto: *Antoni Gaudí.* Milan, 1982.

PEVSNER, Nikolaus: *Pioneros del Diseño Moderno: de William Morris a Walter Gropius.* Buenos Aires, 2000.

PI DE CABANYES, Oriol: *Cases modernistes de Catalunya.* Barcelona, 1992.

PLA, Josep: *Homenots.* Barcelona, 1956.

PUIG-BOADA, Isidre: *El pensament de Gaudí.* Barcelona, 1981.

QUETGLAS, Josep: *Pasado a limpio, ll.* Valencia, 1999.

RÀFOLS, Josep Francesc: *Gaudí: 1852-1926.* Barcelona, 1952.

SOLÀ-MORALES, Ignasi de: *Arquitectura modernista: Fi de segle a Barcelona.* Barcelona, 1992.

STERNER, Gabriele: *Modernismos.* Barcelona, 1982.

TORII, Tokutoshi: *El mundo enigmático de Gaudí,* 2 vols. Madrid, 1983.

TSCHUDI MADSEN, Stephan: *Art Nouveau.* Madrid, 1967.

YÁNIZ, Juan Pedro: *El derribo de la Biblioteca de Filosofía…: La Sagrada Familia es el edificio más valorado,* in *ABC.* Barcelona, 19 August, 1997

GAUDÍ AND THE CRITICS

«It is tremendously sad to see three architects (since the editor himself is an architect) write and publish a book dedicated to the study of the works of an eccentric whose taste is utterly ridiculous. And to say that we must take care in making any reference to the aberrations of our 1900 style which, in view of the lucubrations of the author of the Sagrada Familia, are good sense in person.

»Gaudí is the architect who has dishonoured the city of Barcelona with his numerous constructions that are a disgrace to all those who have trusted in him.

»In his youth, Gaudí built buildings that are true «cocktails» of the strangest styles. In his maturity he began to plagiarise buildings of the Far East without any intelligence or understanding of the most elementary laws of architecture. Finally, to crown his noble career, the idea of building a church in Barcelona whose uncommonly large proportions are explained by the author's humble desire to house the entire Holy Family has been put into his head. This church, already under construction, is the most ridiculous that one can imagine.

»For the authors of the book the logic of Gaudí's buildings and his profound knowledge of architectural laws are a great and good example. But Gaudí has never understood the meaning of statics in construction, nor has he ever taken into account the most elementary bases of architectural art. In my opinion, to make slanting Doric columns bear the weight of the buildings, to make brave tortoises hold up columns that seem to be detached from the floor, to accumulate without any reason, simply for the pleasure of satisfying his imagination, a whole load of construction difficulties is to arrogantly despise or ignore everything that man has painstakingly but gloriously established.

»The most incredible of all is to see how the Spanish clergy, who in spite of everything cannot be unaware of the magnificent architectural tradition of their country, entrust the House of God to an eccentric. But, above all, what can one think of the three architects that have greatly praised absurdities that hardly deserve the slightest mention in the gossip column.»

Christian Zervos, *Cahiers d'Art* (1929)

———◆–▶◀–◆———

«Gaudí is one of the most universal Catalonians that have existed in our history (…) a calculator, a sharp mathematician, a constructor of pure rationality. (…) But, apart from being a constructor, Gaudí was a great artist, a fanatic of plastic beauty, ultrasensitive of forms and the colours of life.»

Josep Pla, *Homenots* (1956)

———◆–▶◀–◆———

«Antonio Gaudí's power as an architect lies in his prolific invention of forms. The variety and expressiveness of the latter as sculptures would only distinguish him as a remarkable modern artist. But they were, in fact, the result of unusual structural resources, of an imaginative display of materials and a unique sense of decoration, three traditional characteristics of a master builder. If we add to this his ability with intangible aspects of architecture such as space, colour and light, one can understand why the architectural world today is so devoted to his relatively few and almost forgotten works.»

George R. Collins, *Antonio Gaudí* (1960)

———◆–▶◀–◆———

«As a synthesis of Gaudí's multiple and prolific performance, after having analysed his life and work, we must highlight the exemplarity of both, which should impress any sensitive spirit that knows them. I find it extremely difficult to find a similar case of such integral and balanced professional dedication as that of this genius. Let his edifying exemplarity and the mark of his steps guide those who feel worthy of emulating him.»

César Martinell, *Gaudí: su vida, su teoría, su obra* (1967)

«Art Nouveau appeared in Spain in a very different way. It was not a tendency, but rather the personal and imaginative architectural expression of a single man: Antonio Gaudí Cornet, who worked in a specific geographical area, Barcelona, the capital of Catalonia. (...) His architecture, simply, has to be experienced: it produces a tremendous impact.

»When attempting to situate his work historically, it must be understood that his was the most original contribution to Art Nouveau architecture. The architectonic conception of the style was never so accomplished as here. Furthermore, Gaudí triumphed where many before him, in the History of Architecture, had failed.»

Stephan Tschudi Madsen, *Art Nouveau* (1967)

«Gaudí's work, elevated with the sorrows and the visions of a genius, is a continuous and experimental search carried out with the tenacity of a superior human being who has left us with something apparently simple, but which, after numerous corrections, contains 'fragments that satisfy generations', just like Leonardo da Vinci or Michelangelo, in the long and difficult process of an extensive and successful artistic creation, but which partly makes up for the loneliness of a man who has loved a lot and has reached old age having lost those relatives who had lived with him.»

Isidre Puig-Boada, *El pensament de Gaudí* (1981)

«Gaudí's professional conduct –extensive in time, intense in execution, fruitful and remarkable in results– would begin the same year in which he received his architect's diploma, lasting until minutes before the accident that would cost him his life. A long road, full of creative activity, from those first works for the Cooperativa Obrera Mataronense until his death half a century later.

»One of Gaudí's main characteristics would be his ability to develop his work more and more to perfection. His practical-mindedness, his orderly, reflexive and logical character, dialectically open to the influence of his most intimate collaborators, would be the main determinant of this ever-evolving activity which his architecture represents. Above the impact that his star moments may have – 'manifesto works', structural inventions, the Güell Palace, the Batlló and Milà houses, the Sagrada Familia church, etc. -, his overall work will be characterised as being like an inexhaustible spring, an ever-flowing river. In those cases which are especially creative or anticipatory, as well as in others which, apparently, are closer to more conventional solutions, the evolutionary process - evident or underlying - that represents Gaudinian architecture will never be interrupted or stopped. (...) Gaudí, the author of ingenious advances, the discoverer of new horizons and roads, will never stop being in step with the times.»

Carlos Flores, *Gaudí, Jujol y el Modernismo catalán* (1982)

«Many a controversy has been raised regarding the architect's personality. Nevertheless, we must admit that we are faced with one of the greatest innovators of 20th -century architecture and that is all thanks to the works he has left us, since his written testimony is minimum.»

Xavier Güell, *Antoni Gaudí* (1986)

«Nowadays, Gaudí's architecture is known and admired all over the world. Numerous books and articles have been published and exhibitions and seminars have been held everywhere.

»Besides, Gaudí is an architect admired by the professionals of architecture, and also by the people and by children. Even when great experts in the History of Architecture have written about his work, the direct understanding of his style and his way of building deserve a simple and concise explanation, which is not based on aesthetic criteria or on the principles deriving from the History of Architecture.

»The Gaudinian ways of construction move away from those produced by the different historical styles over the centuries.

»In spite of the great number of writings and books that have been published, it is not possible to have a full and complete knowledge of Gaudí, because one must study him otherwise, with other methods that are not those of historiography and aesthetics. (…) Gaudí was contemporary to Art Nouveau, but his style cannot be included within the narrow Modernist limits, nor can it be included in any other historical style.

»In Barcelona, Majorca, and Comillas, the poetry of his works continues to be proclaimed, as well as the personality of a creator that had the humble greatness of knowing how to read the purest lessons of architecture in the forms of the three kingdoms of Nature.»

Juan Bassegoda, *El Gran Gaudí* (1989)

«It may well be said that Barcelona was fortunate enough to have had this important character of contemporary art, within the extraordinarily lively context of the last quarter of the century. (…) He had an intuitive and passionate vision of the world of architecture as total art: Gaudí's project was that of an entire epoch.»

François Loyer, *Cataluña modernista: 1888-1929* (1991)

«His pretension of profound truth is what has given Gaudí and the whole Gaudinian tradition their arrogant superiority, their estrangement from the History of Architecture of the rest of mortals.»

Ignasi de Solà-Morales, *Arquitectura modernista: fi de segle a Barcelona* (1992)

«Gaudí was a humble human being who was endowed with a sharp aesthetic instinct, a man possessed by a great rapture of the spirit, by some solid creative deliriums. And we must consider him, above all, as a visually ingenious being.»

Oriol Pi de Cabanyes, *Cases modernistes de Catalunya* (1992)

«Gaudí dies in 1926; three years later, in 1929, Mies van der Rohe comes to Barcelona and greets King Alfonso XIII with a top hat. Gaudí and Mies came so close to meeting one another. A missed opportunity or simply, impossible continuity. (…) There is a great architectural void in Spain around 1920, only broken by the continuity of the work of the great genius Antoni Gaudí.»

María Teresa Muñoz, *La otra arquitectura orgánica* (1995)

———————◆◆◀◆————————

«The way to approach Gaudí (1852-1926) is more complicated: one must start by first clearing the dense Barcelona mythology that surrounds and suffocates his figure.

»My advice would be to forget about books, postcards etc. –however square and Modernist they may be– and go directly to visit his works –if they were not so modified regarding the original project, construction and location–. The best thing to do would be to begin with photographs of that period, comparing and completing them with the occasional visit to the work in question.»

Josep Quetglas, *Pasado a limpio, II* (1999)

———————◆◆◀◆————————

ALPHABETICAL INDEX OF WORKS

A

Artigas Gardens, 52, 52, 83

B

Bellesguard, 10, 45, 46, 47, 76
Bust of Antoni Gaudí, 6

C

Casa Batlló, 49, 50, 51, 68, 69, 70, 71, 71, 74, 76
Casa Botines, 32, 33, 76
Casa Calvet, 37, 37, 38, 70, 70, 71, 76, 88
Casa dels Ossos, see Casa Batlló
Casa El Capricho, 18, 18, 19, 72, 74
Casa Fernández y Andrés, see Casa Botines

Casa Figueras, see Bellesguard
Casa Milà, 6, 8, 9, 48, 53, 54, 55, 68, 68, 70, 71, 76, 78, 80, 84, 85, 87
Casa Vicens, 14, 15, 16, 17, 71, 74

E

Episcopal Palace, 26, 27, 28, 29

G

Güell Colony Church Crypt, 39, 40, 41, 79, 84, 84
Güell Palace, 13, 22, 22, 23, 24, 25, 76, 76, 82
Güell Park, 12, 36, 42, 43, 44, 73, 84, 89
Güell Stables, 20, 20, 21, 73, 74, 75
Güell Wine Cellars, 34, 34, 35, 76

P

Pedrera, La, see Casa Milà

S

Sagrada Familia Church, 58, 58, 59, 60, 61, 62, 63, 64, 65, 66, 67, 69, 74
Sagrada Familia Provisional School, 56, 56, 57, 86

T

Teresian School, 29, 30, 31, 32, 76